W9-CBB-968

ONE·HOUR
COLLEGE APPLICATION ESSAY

write your college admission essay today

JAN MELNIK

DATE DUE

FEB 2 4 2010	
OCT 0 1 2010	
FEB 0 7 2011	
AUG 2 3 2011	
SEP 1 7 2014	

ONE-HOUR COLLEGE APPLICATION ESSAY

© 2008 by Jan Melnik

Published by JIST Works, an imprint of JIST Publishing, Inc.
8902 Otis Avenue
Indianapolis, IN 46216-1033
Phone: 1-800-648-JIST   Fax: 1-800-JIST-FAX   E-mail: info@jist.com

Visit our Web site at www.jist.com for information on JIST, free job search tips, book chapters, and ordering instructions for our many products!

Quantity discounts are available for JIST books. Have future editions of JIST books automatically delivered to you on publication through our convenient standing order program. Please call our Sales Department at 1-800-648-5478 for a free catalog and more information.

Trade Product Manager: Lori Cates Hand
Interior Designer: Aleata Howard
Cover Designer: Katy Bodenmiller
Proofreaders: Linda Seifert, Jeanne Clark
Indexer: Kelly D. Henthorne

Printed in the United States of America
12 11 10 09 08 07   9 8 7 6 5 4 3 2 1

Library of Congress Cataloging-in-Publication Data

Melnik, Jan.
    One-hour college application essay : write your college admission essay
    today / Jan Melnik.
        p. cm.
    Includes index.
    ISBN 978-1-59357-475-8 (alk. paper)
    1. College applications--United States. 2. Universities and
    colleges--United States--Admission. I. Title.
    LB2351.52.U6M45 2008
    378.1'616--dc22

                                                        2007027290

All rights reserved. No part of this book may be reproduced in any form or by any means, or stored in a database or retrieval system, without prior written permission of the publisher except in the case of brief quotations embodied in articles or reviews. Making copies of any part of this book for any purpose other than your own personal use is a violation of United States copyright laws. For permission requests, please contact the Copyright Clearance Center at www.copyright.com or (978) 750-8400.

We have been careful to provide accurate information in this book, but it is possible that errors and omissions have been introduced. Please consider this in making any college plans or other important decisions. Trust your own judgment above all else and in all things.

Trademarks: All brand names and product names used in this book are trade names, service marks, trademarks, or registered trademarks of their respective owners.

ISBN 978-1-59357-475-8

ACC Library Services
Austin, Texas

About This Book

*O*ne-Hour College Application Essay is a complete resource that provides valuable information to high school juniors and seniors. Many students claim that writing an application essay is one of the most stressful activities that they faced in high school, and especially with regard to the college admissions process.

This book attempts to dispel the anxiety associated with essay writing by providing straightforward advice from the perspectives of college admission deans and new college students alike (the latter of whom share their in-depth experiences and advice about writing application essays).

For those who need to write an essay quickly, chapter 4 provides a one-hour blueprint for getting the job done. Get your stopwatch ready; this is exactly the game plan you'll need!

But taking things in logical order, chapter 1 explains fully how the application essay is used and why it is so important for most schools. There's also a handy timetable for the various methods of application (from Early Decision and Early Action to rolling admissions and everything in between).

Admissions experts weigh in on every facet of the application process, providing in-depth viewpoints about the application essay in particular in chapter 2. You'll find their do's and don'ts to be especially helpful when selecting essay topics and working through the writing process.

Chapter 3 shares additional expert admissions advice, including a selection of handpicked essays. There is also up-to-date information on the trends admissions deans are seeing with respect to admission and college attendance.

Chapter 5 augments the one-hour essay-writing formula shared in chapter 4 with its detailed advice from college students. There are additional worksheets to use for essay writing as well as dozens of actual essay questions gleaned from colleges and universities across the country.

While the emphasis in this book is on the application essay, it makes sense to look at the whole admissions process. Chapter 6 describes all the many components that make up a college application package. The chapter includes in-depth information on everything from standardized testing to letters of recommendation.

Chapter 7 is a collection of actual unedited essays written by high school juniors and seniors who now attend a wide spectrum of institutions nationwide. They cover a broad range of interesting topics. These students' insights will prove especially useful if you are still deciding about which topics you will write.

Finally, in the appendix you'll meet the admissions deans, directors, advisors, and vice presidents who generously shared their collective experience and advice throughout this book.

Good luck embarking on the college selection process. May you find much help and inspiration in these pages to assist you specifically with the essay-writing portion of your college application.

Acknowledgments

This book would not have been possible without the collective input, guidance, and expertise of two important groups of people. First of all, I am grateful to the college students who so willingly shared their own stories, the essays they wrote, and their experiences about the entire college-search process in general—and their application efforts in particular. Your collective experiences are inspiring and I wish each of you the very best in the continuation of your studies and in all future endeavors.

Secondly, I am deeply indebted to the dedicated admissions deans, directors of admission, admission counselors, and vice presidents of student enrollment/admissions who graciously answered my many questions, offered their substantial wisdom and guidance, and provided illuminating insights into the entire admissions process. Future undergraduates can rest assured that the advice and counsel provided herein will be instrumental to their success in creating authentic application packages that truly reflect the best they have to offer.

I'm also very appreciative of the efforts of several others: I had the privilege of working with an exceptional editor in Lori Cates Hand, who helped me shape the development of this project with her direction and expertise. A special thanks for accommodating my writing schedule is in order to my German professor and now dear friend, Veronika Hofstaetter. Two of my sons, twins Dan and Wes, were willing "guinea pigs" as I experimented with various survey instruments probing the applications process. They were equally agreeable about sharing their own stories, which you'll find interspersed throughout the book (at press time, they are college sophomores). As always, my husband, Ron, was supportive throughout the months of extensive research and writing time that I spent in creating this work. Finally, as our youngest son, Stephen, enters his senior year in high school, I hope he'll glean considerable value and direction from the key nuggets of wisdom and practical, salient advice offered by the generosity of successful students who have gone before him and from the admissions professionals at respected universities around the country.

Contents

Chapter 3: More Advice from the Admission Pros: Assistance, Feedback, Examples, and Trends 45

Chapter 4: Quick Steps for Crafting an Essay in an Hour 63

© JIST Works

© JIST Works

© JIST Works

A Brief Introduction to Using This Book

This book is intended to accomplish several objectives:

- Remove some of the anxiety surrounding the essay-writing process—humanizing the approach so that you recognize the value (and importance!) of being 100 percent honest, authentic, and yourself in crafting your essay.

- Provide meaningful, useful tools to help prompt you to get started and get out of writer's-block mode.

- Offer inspiration and encouragement by sharing success stories from a wide range of students. Although many of the students participating in this project are high achievers (top 5 percent of class, valedictorian, and so on), there is a good mix as well among average-but-accomplished, high-average-and-motivated, and even a few slightly sub-average-but-distinguished-in-other-ways students who have found success pursuing admission to the college "of their dreams" that best meets their academic, intellectual, and other needs.

- Provide factual advice about the role the essay plays within a variety of institutions. In only a few situations do the essays matter little. Most schools place a fairly significant emphasis on the quality of the essay. A dean of admissions told me recently that an essay came into play for him in making a "no" decision on a candidate that was right on the fence in terms of academic qualifications. Had the essay been well-written and, at least, properly proofread and grammatically correct, the outcome might have been different.

- Give expert advice from a diverse group of admissions professionals (recognizing that there is not a one-size-fits-all-mentality here; rather, the collective expertise and wisdom from experts will provide a solid foundation for understanding what institutions are likely seeking).

- Provide real-life advice from more than 40 college students, many of whom completed their own college application essays just one year ago. Their successes, advice, wisdom, and even mistakes will prove very helpful to high school juniors and seniors just beginning their college-search and application essay-writing journey.

- Discuss the full process of good writing: idea generation and brain-storming, outlining, draft writing, and multiple rewrite sessions. The book also shares key details about the importance of proofreading, editing, double- and triple-checking work, and having several trusted advisor-readers (English teachers, for example).

As long as colleges and universities—as well as the Common Application—continue to require an essay or subtly encourage its use on an optional basis, I believe students can benefit by reading a range of essay examples, by reading peer-level advice about the entire process, and by reading expert opinions representing a wide range of beliefs from admissions professionals from a variety of institutions. And that's exactly what you'll get from this book.

© JIST Works

Chapter 1

Why You Need a Terrific Essay

Why do you need a terrific essay? In a few words: The college admissions process can be extremely competitive. This chapter gives you some background on the admissions process, shows how the essay fits in, and tells you why a terrific essay is so important.

A Little Background About the Admissions Process

Consider a few of the numbers. There are more than 3,800 four-year colleges and universities nationwide and over 1,000 two-year institutions. According to the United States Census Bureau, in October 2005, there were approximately 11 million full-time undergraduate students at institutions around the United States (an additional 3.5 million undergraduate students were attending college on a part-time basis). This translates into some 4.1 million students in the most recent freshman class for which nationwide statistics are available.

And the incoming freshman classes of 2008, 2009, 2010, and beyond are expected to be even bigger. These students attend a wide range of institutions—from public to military and private; from rural to suburban and urban; from very small and small to mid-size and large in terms of student populations; and from affordable to very expensive, to name just a few of the characteristics.

Importantly, these colleges and universities admit students in a variety of ways: from rolling or open admissions to regular admissions with a specific deadline and via Early Action and/or Early Decision (explanations about the different types of admissions appear later in this chapter). Admission to some of these schools is highly selective, representing the top academic tier of institutions throughout the country (including the original Ivy League institutions as well as institutions earning more recent status as "New Ivy Leaguers"). Admission to others may be considered quite selective, selective, not as selective, and not selective. For a school that is not selective, nearly all applicants meeting published admission criteria are accepted. For a school that is highly selective, admission rates might be as restrictive as 1 in 10 or 1 in 20 (in other words, for every 20 students who apply, just one is accepted).

Admissions Criteria

Nearly every college and university today publishes admissions criteria and facts about recently admitted classes on their Web sites. You can also seek this information through the college's admissions office. Of interest to most students are details concerning the number of applicants in a typical year, the percentage of applicants actually accepted, and the number ultimately choosing to attend that institution (called *yield* in admissions parlance). For instance, a college of 4,000 undergraduate students might receive 5,000 applications and consider itself to be selective in terms of acceptances (in other words, not highly selective but not the least selective, either). Perhaps 50 percent of applicants will be accepted, 2,500 in this case. Of that number, perhaps 1,000 will ultimately enroll and make up next year's freshman class. This data is frequently published on an institution's Web site (see the following sidebar).

Acceptance Information Colleges Publish
Your Typical University—Anywhere, USA

Number of Freshman Applications: 5,301

Acceptance Rate: 43 percent (2,279 students)

Number of First-Years: 620 (students actually attending)

In addition to this statistical data with regard to acceptance, most schools publish the average SAT and/or ACT scores of its most recently admitted class or a score range (more detailed information about the SAT and ACT appears later in this chapter). For example, the school might indicate the following:

Average SAT Scores Among Applicant Pool: 1275 (Math: 640/Verbal: 635)

Average SAT Scores Among Admitted Students: 1335 (Math: 665/Verbal: 670)

Average SAT Scores Among First-Years: 1299 (Math: 647/Verbal: 652)

Average ACT Score Among Applicant Pool: 29

Average ACT Score Among Admitted Students: 32

Average ACT Score Among First-Years: 31

© JIST Works

This information is often published using a range or reflecting the middle 50 percent of the respective student population. For instance, a school might say that the SAT scores for First-Years were as follows: SAT middle 50 percent is 545–625 M and 535–625 V. This means that fully 50 percent of the student population enrolled as first-year students had SAT Math scores falling somewhere between 545 and 625 and SAT Verbal scores falling between 535 and 625. To a prospective student, this means that 25 percent of the first-year students attending that school have SAT scores above those levels—and 25 percent have SAT scores below those levels.

ACT scores and GPA (Grade Point Average) may also be reported in a similar manner using a range:

ACT middle 50 percent: 25–29

Average GPA: 3.1 out of 4.0

Expert opinions vary significantly, but you should consider that if your SAT or ACT scores fall within the range that 50 percent of attending first-years do, this could be a reasonable fit; in other words, a *target school*. If your scores fall below that 50th percentile range, you might consider the school to be a *reach*. Finally, if your scores are above the 50th percentile range, you might possibly consider the school to be a *safety*. SAT and/or ACT scores are just one or two of the measures college admissions professionals evaluate; a variety of other factors are discussed throughout this book, including the all-important essay that comprises the bulk of this book's content. But if you are wise, you will include schools in all categories when applying and not select only those schools with published scores that far exceed your results or, by the same token, that are all below your achievement level.

How Schools Show Rank

Colleges typically indicate the high school class rank of their first-year students using percentages:

- Those Students Ranked in Top 5% of Class: 2%
- Those Students Ranked in Top 10% of Class: 6%
- Those Students Ranked in Top 25% of Class: 18%
- Those Students Ranked in Top 50% of Class: 62%
- Those Students Ranked in Top 75% of Class: 92%

Class rank might also be published like this:

- 64% in top 10%
- 85% in top 20%
- 93% in top 50%

When assessing your chances of acceptance, if your class rank were in the bottom 25 percent, this particular school (with just 7 percent of the accepted student population falling into the bottom 50 percent of the class) would most certainly be a reach considering only this criteria.

Other Valuable Information on the College

You can find other valuable information among the fact data usually published on a college's admissions Web site. This often includes the following details:

- Diversity and ethnic background of students

- Number of states and countries from which students come to the school

- Number of students participating in on-campus clubs, activities, and varsity athletics

- Percentage of students receiving merit awards (scholarships or grants that do not need to be paid back) and financial support in the form of student loans and work-study opportunities

- The ratio of men to women; and the ratio of students to faculty

- The percentage of students studying abroad

- The retention rates (how many students return after their freshman year—and how many students graduate at four years, five years, and beyond)

- Percentage of students by major

- Percentage of students by classes of differing sizes (75 percent of students in classes with fewer than 20 students each; 10 percent of students in classes with 21 to 45 students; 10 percent of students in classes with 46 to 74 students; 4 percent of students in classes with 75 to 99 students; and 1 percent of students in classes with 100 or more members)

© JIST Works

All of these numbers should not be discouraging: Keep in mind that although study results vary, most experts in academia state that the majority of freshmen do attend the college that was first on their list. Actual numbers range from the high 60s to nearly 80 percent in terms of percentage of college freshmen attending their first-choice school. Obviously, the savvy student applies to more than one school. With the advent of the Common Application (more about this in chapter 6), students can more easily apply to more schools. It is not uncommon for students to apply to eight, ten, or even more schools. However, there is great value (to say nothing of saved application fees, wherein one application might be as much as $50 to $65) in applying to very carefully selected schools that cross the spectrum of safety, target, and reach.

How Many Applications to Send? And to Which Schools?

The majority of college admissions professionals consulted suggest the following strategy:

- Students should submit one or two applications to colleges that are considered safety schools.
- They should apply to several reach schools.
- The majority of applications (perhaps two to five) should be to target schools.

How Should I Choose Where to Apply?

Something important to keep in mind: Don't apply to a school that you wouldn't want to attend. This seems obvious, but in a quest to select several safety schools, some students don't spend sufficient time choosing viable options. In addition, anecdotal evidence seems to suggest that many students don't even visit their safety schools. This is not the best plan; although it might not always be possible to visit every school on your wish list, safety schools, in particular, are frequently located within a reasonable distance of your home and, therefore, should warrant a visit before being added to the pool of potential contenders.

Another recommendation on this point is to be absolutely sure that there is a good range reflected in the schools you're targeting. One very accomplished student who shares a personal application story later in this book (along with a great essay), targeted only reach schools at the top of his achievement spectrum. Despite being an exceptional candidate, he was rejected by all but one. Fortunately, he loves the school and has enjoyed his experience. Nonetheless, it might have been nice to have had a choice among several schools, along with the benefit of perusing several different financial package offers that accompany the acceptances.

Remember that the Ivy league schools (Yale, Harvard, Dartmouth, Brown, Princeton, Columbia, Cornell, and the University of Pennsylvania—and Stanford, considered the Ivy league school on the West Coast) typically accept under 20 percent of their applicants. This compares to an average of between 65 and 70 percent of applicants to all other colleges and universities in the United States.

Another key statistic to keep in mind is that the Ivy League institutions traditionally do not *accept* some 50 to 55 percent of valedictorians who apply. Does this mean that if you are not the school valedictorian that you should not even bother with applying to an Ivy League? Of course not. For instance, Dartmouth College reports on its admissions Web site that the profile of the Class of 2010, with a little over 1,000 freshmen, comprised 30 percent valedictorians and 10.6 percent salutatorians (meaning that 60 percent of the class did not attain that lofty status).

As a final note on the highly competitive college admissions experiences with Ivy League schools, you should also note that fewer than *three-tenths of one percent* of freshmen at colleges and universities around the United States are enrolled at an Ivy. Although these schools provide outstanding educations, they are not alone in that achievement; there are literally hundreds of excellent institutions providing exceptional educations to a wide range of students across the country, including some of the brightest and highest-achieving students from around the world.

Find the School That's Right for You!

What is most important is to focus on finding the school that is best for you with respect to academic program, environment (location, size, type, and feel of campus), rigor of curriculum, student-to-faculty ratio, opportunities for extracurricular programs (art, sports, music, and so on), study-abroad opportunities, internship experiences, and myriad other factors that are important to weigh.

So Where Does the Essay Fit In?

By the time you are a high school senior, the essay remains the one item over which you can have the greatest influence. Gil Villanueva, the Dean of Admissions at Brandeis University, stated that "aside from your

© JIST Works

senior-year performance, your essay is the only part of the college admission process you are able to fully control. Until you have been extended offers of admission, the ball is in the admission committee's court. While a good essay can only help you, a poorly written essay will surely hinder your candidacy."

When high school seniors are preparing their college applications, the grades on the transcripts on which they'll be judged are fairly well cast in stone. These students have probably completed at least two rounds of the SAT or ACT test and may have taken one or more SAT Subject Tests (formerly called SAT-II Subject Tests). Although a high school senior might take a final SAT or ACT in October, the numbers "are what they are," as is commonly said. Of course, these same students do have control on the teachers and others that they identify for writing letters of recommendation (but they have no influence over the content of those letters).

Therefore, the essay remains the single most important item over which you can truly make a final, meaningful effort. It is thus one of the most angst-filled activities related to college admissions that there is.

Somewhat paradoxically, the essay does not rank as the top criteria by most schools (often, it is no higher than fourth in a long line of criteria considered by most institutions). It might even be relegated much lower on the list or considered optional by some schools. However, the serious-minded student still wants to put forth his or her best effort with a quality, authentic essay that resonates with uniqueness about their individual capabilities, interests, or passions.

Timetable for the College Admissions Process

There are several milestone events related to college admissions: completion of standardized testing, determining the optimal time to apply to a school, and developing/completing your application essays. This section briefly visits the testing and application timing concerns first before delving into the essay.

Although some students (and their helicopter parents) begin thinking and planning for college as early as the middle-school years, most students actively engage in the process during their junior year in high school. Of course, the foundation they establish as freshmen and sophomores in high school is very important. But the real work typically begins during the junior year with taking PSATs, registering for SAT or ACT prep courses, possibly taking skills/interest inventories, and making preliminary college visits—all while thinking about the big question: "What do I *think* I want to be/do—and study in college?"

Virtually all students will benefit by maintaining a document (a working resume, if you will) of accomplishments, highlights, organizational involvement, and achievements throughout their high school years. This material often becomes the grist used in preparing actual college applications, is very helpful for all people who will be asked to write letters of recommendation, and may possibly accompany an application.

Over the course of the junior and senior years in high school, students begin visiting college campuses, attending college fairs, and participating in college open houses. You should keep in mind that the best time to visit a college campus—to get a real feel for the flavor of the school itself—is when college classes are in session. Summer may be convenient for your family to plan visits, but you'll miss seeing campuses at their busiest.

SAT and ACT Testing Information

Because standardized test scores are essential to many college applications, it makes sense to pay attention to the timing of these tests and their value as part of the overall application. Many students today find that it makes sense to take both the SAT and the ACT. Each test plays to different strengths (including test-taking preferences). Nearly all schools will consider best performance on a given test (so that if you take the SAT in January of your junior year and again in June, the best individual scores will be accepted—say, 630 Mathematics in January and 590 Critical Reading in June).

As you are working on polishing your essays, remember that there are early deadlines for registering for the final fall test dates for both the ACT and SAT that will still allow scores to be considered as part of your application. Details about these two tests follow.

© JIST Works

SAT® Reasoning Test

The SAT Reasoning Test is sponsored by the College Board (www.collegeboard.com). It has been in existence—with a number of modifications—since 1900. Originally called the Scholastic Achievement Test, it subsequently was called the Scholastic Aptitude Test and then evolved to its current name, the Scholastic Assessment Test. It is most commonly referred to as the SAT Reasoning Test. SATs are administered seven times each year at certain schools around the United States to more than two million high school students annually and are accepted by many universities and colleges nationwide.

Scores are reported for each of the three subject areas (Mathematics, Critical Reading, and Writing) on a scale of 200 to 800 each. Hence, the minimum score on the SAT is a 600; the maximum score is 2400. There are a range of multiple-choice, writing, and response questions. The Writing section requires students to produce an essay on a specified topic in 25 minutes and is evaluated as a subscore; there is also a multiple-choice writing subscore reported as part of the overall number. The total test time is just under four hours with breaks included.

Prior to 2005, the SAT comprised just two sections: Mathematics and Verbal. Today, most universities are still not officially considering the Writing score (many admissions offices indicate that until the Writing test has been around at least five years with historical scoring data, it really cannot be effectively evaluated as a measure for admission). Therefore, a number of college selection guides that publish median SAT performance are showing the sum of scores for just the Mathematics and Critical Reading tests.

SAT Subject Tests are also offered by the College Board. These are available in a wide range of topical areas for students who have mastery of specific subjects and wish to have a more in-depth measure of their competency. You can take up to three SAT Subject Tests on one test day (but not on the same day as the SAT Reasoning Test).

The 2006–2007 fee for taking the SAT Reasoning Test was $41.50. The fee to register for an SAT Subject Test was $18; each additional Subject Test's fee was $8.

ACT® Test

The ACT (American College Testing program), a college admission and placement examination, is also accepted by many colleges and universities nationwide (www.act.org). The test was introduced in 1959 and is taken by more than two million students throughout the United States each year. The test is available at high schools five times each year (with an additional testing period available in some schools).

The ACT test is based on curricula taught in high schools in the subject areas of English, reading, mathematics, and science; a writing component is also available. As with the SAT, students may take the ACT as many times as desired. Most students take the test in their junior year; many retake the test in their senior year.

ACT scores follow a scale of 1 to 36 in each of the four test areas. The four individual test scores are then averaged to create a composite score; this highest composite score is 36. The component tests range in time from 35 minutes (reading and science) to 45 minutes (English) and 60 minutes (mathematics); with breaks, the total is just under four hours. The writing test adds an incremental 30 minutes to the overall test time.

The 2006–2007 fee for taking the ACT was $29. The fee to take the ACT Plus Writing test was $43.

Types of Application Decisions: When and How to Apply

While you're working on your essay (see the sidebar on page 19 in this chapter for the recommended best time to write yours), be mindful of when you plan to submit your complete college application to the schools you have selected. There are a variety of application types and deadlines available at most schools. Terms that you'll frequently encounter are *Single-Choice Early Action, Early Decision, Early Action, Regular Decision,* and *Rolling Admission* (along with several variations of a few of these). In the recent five or so years, there has been some shake-up within

Note: *With the exception of Early Decision, which is detailed later, the National Common Reply Date for students to communicate their decision to attend a particular school and provide a financial commitment in the form of a deposit is* **May 1.** *For all but Early Decision applicants, this means that whether you receive your acceptance in December or April, you have until May 1 to definitely make up your mind and bind that decision with a deposit. Of course, students can bind their decision as early as they wish, following receipt of their acceptance, and do not need to wait until May 1 to send in their acceptance and deposit.*

© JIST Works

some of the top schools in the country—with some schools abolishing Early Decision altogether, some incorporating the newer Single-Choice Early Action, and some simply waiting it out to see how the dust settles.

Table 1.1 is a glossary of terms—and the estimated timetable for each application type. You should also visit the Web sites of schools in which you are interested to learn the types of admission available and the actual deadlines.

Table 1.1: Types of Applications at a Glance		
Type of Application	*Typical Deadline*	*Who Is This Right For?*
Single-Choice Early Action… Nonbinding	November 1	You have a top choice—and don't want to apply Early Decision/early action anywhere else *but* don't want to be obligated to attend.
Early Decision… Binding	November 1 to November 15	You have absolutely one top choice and want to go only there if accepted.
Early Decision II… Binding	January 1 to January 15	If you have a preferred second choice (and were rejected early from your first) *or* you are late on your applications, but this is your number-one choice.
Early Action… Nonbinding	November 1	You want the security of getting an Early Decision or two from one or more schools you'd really like to attend, but want to keep options open.
Regular Decision… Nonbinding	December 15 to January 31	You're not in a hurry to know of acceptance (often you won't hear until the beginning of April).
Rolling Admission… Nonbinding	Usually no deadline	You will typically hear within several weeks if you do choose to apply early (November–December); it's nice to have one or two acceptances from schools early in the process.

The following sections describe these admission types in more detail.

Single-Choice Early Action

A relatively new "flavor" in the menu of college application timelines, some highly competitive schools have instituted Single-Choice Early Action (for instance, it is offered at Stanford, Harvard, and Yale, to name a few). Application deadlines are typically November 1. Although it is nonbinding and students who are accepted do not need to commit until May 1, they are prohibited from applying via Early Decision or Early Action at any other school. Acceptance, deferral, or rejection is provided by the middle of December. (A deferral means that you will not get an official decision until April.)

Because of the timing of this application and its early deadline, you will not have the option of having your first-quarter/semester senior grades or the results of any late-fall SAT or ACT testing considered. There are a few exceptions: The October ACT test results would probably be available in time to accompany an application, and November SAT II Subject Tests would also be likely to provide results in time for consideration.

Early Decision

As with Single-Choice Early Action, this form of application is for students who have determined the one school that they absolutely, positively want to attend—it's their number-one choice and they would plan to go there if accepted. The application deadline is usually **November 1.** This is considered a binding application; that is, if you are accepted by an early-decision school *and the accompanying offer package (including financials) is acceptable,* you are expected to attend. Under the honor system, students are to apply via Early Decision to just one institution (of course, if you receive a rejection and there is still time, you can apply to another institution by Early Decision after that rejection). In addition, students who have applied to other schools via Regular, Early Action, or Rolling Admission concurrent with the one Early-Decision application are expected to immediately withdraw those applications if they receive early-decision acceptance. Note that some Early-Decision schools prohibit students from applying to other schools via Early Action. Payment of a deposit is generally required a few weeks following an early-decision acceptance.

This form of admission is ideal for students who believe they know exactly what they want to do and where they want to go. Decisions are generally

© JIST Works

rendered by the end of December (and, frequently, at the beginning or middle of December).

Early Decision (II)

Not as prevalent, colleges that offer Early Decision may offer a second period of Early Decision called Early Decision II. It works in the same manner as the traditional version described in the preceding paragraphs, but with a different set of application deadlines. For many, the Early Decision II deadline is moved to somewhere between January 1 and 15, with decisions provided by the middle to end of February. All other conditions as exist for the traditional early-decision process apply.

Early Decision II is a good choice for students who might have been wait-listed or rejected at their number-one choice and have a preferred number-two school "in the wings." There is still the advantage of learning a decision more quickly than in other forms of application, but there is also the obligation to attend if accepted.

Early Action

Often with similar deadlines as Early Decision (traditional), this form of application is considered nonbinding. In other words, students make Early-Action application to their preferred institutions by November 1 and are assured an earlier-than-regular response of acceptance (or rejection), generally as early as December, but continuing into February. There is no obligation to attend (unlike Early Decision).

Early Action may be considered ideal for students who are fairly certain of a few schools that they would like to attend—but do not want to have the constraints of being required to attend one and only one school (as stipulated by Early Decision). Because there is no obligation to accept, there is more flexibility. In addition, for some students, it is reassuring to have one or two acceptances at Early-Action schools of choice early in the process— while perhaps pursuing application at extremely competitive and/or reach schools (for them) later in the application process. As some students have said, "a bird in the hand (early-action acceptance with the knowledge of being accepted at a school you would want to attend) is worth two in the bush (awaiting regular admission to possibly more competitive schools where a student might not be accepted)."

Increasing numbers of colleges and universities nationwide are offering some form of Early Action and/or Early Decision, quite possibly reflective of the continuing competitive atmosphere within the realm of college admissions. Students should not feel pressured to apply early to any institution and should carefully weigh the criteria and advice they receive from multiple sources (parents, counselors, teachers, and advisors). The most important thing is identifying the best fit with one or more colleges and adhering to deadlines posted for the different types of application.

Regular Decision

Probably pursued by more students than any other type of application, deadlines for application generally range from the end of December to the middle or even end of January. A decision from the school is usually promised by the beginning of April. As with nearly all schools except those with Early Decision, a commitment (in the form of a decision with a deposit of anywhere from $200 to $500) is due by the traditional date of May 1.

Regular Decision allows students to produce results their first quarter or semester of senior year—possibly enhancing their application profile. They can also pursue ACT and SAT I and/or Subject testing to post higher scores (most schools will take the highest result in each area from several different tests, so that, for instance, if your math score was highest on a January SAT test, but the verbal score was highest on a June SAT test, both would be considered). Additionally, by applying via Regular Decision, teachers and others contacted to write letters of recommendation will have a longer timeframe in which to know you (important for senior-class teachers meeting students for the first time in September). There are additional opportunities afforded by those few extra months to distinguish performance in other areas—from extracurricular and volunteer involvement to receipt of special achievements or awards.

With Regular Decision, students may apply to as many schools as they wish. Even if an acceptance is provided immediately (January), they are under no obligation to render a decision until the May 1 deadline. Incidentally, many schools will provide students with a card and envelope to use indicating their decision *not* to attend; you are, of course, urged to use this as soon as you have made a decision (it could then release slots available to wait-listed students). For schools that do not provide this mechanism, it is a courtesy to write a brief note to all institutions where you have been accepted with your decision not to attend. It is not necessary to explain details, but most schools appreciate knowing where you decided to attend instead.

© JIST Works

Rolling Admission

You may apply at any time to institutions using Rolling Admissions. There are no early deadlines and you'll receive a prompt decision on your application—often as quickly as just a few weeks after submittal. Although Rolling Admission does not carry an early deadline, students seeking to apply to schools with Rolling Admission and choosing to do so relatively early (November and December) are likely to find themselves with early decisions, just as their formal Early Action– and/or Early Decision–applying high school friends. Again, it can be a significant advantage and boon for a high school senior to receive his or her first acceptance from a school that made the applications list (even if it is not the first-choice school); it's usually a pretty exciting day when the first "fat" envelope arrives!

What's the Reason for an Application Essay?

With the preliminaries about the college admissions process out of the way earlier in this chapter, we can now get into the heart and soul of this book: the college application essay.

As you'll read in this chapter—and especially in chapters 2 and 3, where admission deans provide exceptional insights into the entire applications process as it relates to the essay—the essay plays an integral role in the admissions process. Many admissions experts describe the role of an essay as being able to "paint a picture" or "tell the story" of the applicant. Don Bishop, Associate Vice President for Enrollment Management, Creighton University, described in-depth the role of the application essay:

The essay is the primary voice you have to tell the college about yourself—why you are interested in their school and what interests you. A well-written essay will not only tell the college something important about you that you want them to know—it should also increase their interest in you. The admissions office already has your high school transcript and test results, your list of activities, and your school recommendations where others tell them about you. The essay is your personal opportunity to tell them about what matters to you and who you think you are and who you want to become. No one can tell that story better than you. The other parts of your application will cause the selection team to make assumptions about you based on comparative data from the other applicants. The essay is where the applicant alone has the power to establish a perception of themselves to the reader.

Use **Your** *Voice to Tell Your Story*

According to Gil Villanueva, Dean of Admissions, Brandeis University, "The essay allows you to paint a picture of yourself. It gives life to your application. It is your opportunity to speak to the admissions committee. Let it be your voice and yours alone. While most admissions officers are interested in learning if you can write a good essay, we are also keen on understanding more about you, including gaining insight on your thought processes, values, and interests. Make certain that your essay is well written. This means you have a beginning, middle, and an end. With modern word-processing software, there are no excuses for spelling or overt grammatical errors. Also, know when to use semicolons and commas. Most importantly, write about topics that you are comfortable, knowledgeable, or even excited about. Sometimes a simple subject makes for a terrific essay topic, e.g. the contents of your school locker, the books on your shelf, or the bumper stickers on your car."

Other perspectives regarding the importance of the essay include the following thoughts:

- "We use the essay to *know students better*…what do you want us to know that we will not find in the application?" (Jean Jordan, Interim Dean of Admission, Emory University)

- "The essay is judged differently at all universities. It is important to check with the college one is applying to and learn the weight that the essay holds. In my opinion, the college essay is an effective tool for a student to show an admissions office who he or she is as a person. If a student can do that, he or she will enhance their chances of an admissions staff member pushing for their acceptance, especially if there are two students [of similar backgrounds and credentials] vying for one spot." (Eric Simonelli, Admission Advisor, University of Rhode Island)

- "With the Common Application (CA), most colleges aren't requiring a significant writing sample other than the one prescribed by the CA. This means students can direct their energy toward producing *but one well-crafted piece.* So we look for corroboration of the quality of the writing in the essay throughout the file—in recommendations, grades, scores, and the short-answer responses provided by the student." (Vince Cuseo, Dean of Admission, Occidental College)

- "Essays matter more in an extremely selective admission process (under 20 percent admit rate) because there is a surplus of highly qualified applicants by the numbers. With so many high testers and valedictorians in their pools, ultra-selective colleges have the luxury of picking based on the person revealed through the essay, activities, etc. Intellectual colleges such as Chicago, Swarthmore, and Reed look for a passion for learning, not simply high numbers." (Paul Marthers, Dean of Admission, Reed College)

- "What we are looking for: How will a student add value to Rice University in terms of once they are matriculated? It is important for students to convey that they really understand the specific culture of the university and its subtle nuances. Did the student really investigate the university they are considering? Is this reflected in the essay?" (Chris Muñoz, Vice President for Enrollment, Rice University)

Jeanne Jenkins, the Director of Strategic Initiatives in the Admissions Office of Rensselaer Polytechnic Institute, pointed out the value of the application essay. "In a school that receives 10,000 applications, perhaps as many as 8,000 of them reflect students in the top 10 percent of their class. So, on one hand, you might be tempted to say, 'how wrong can you go' admitting anyone among such a qualified group. On the other hand, we try to admit one student at a time—individually, as human beings—reviewing applications for specific types of information. The essay is a critical part of the process."

When Is the Best Time to Work on Application Essays?

The summer following your junior year in high school is generally considered the best time to work on the application essay(s). If you are engaged in sports, music, and other programs in your senior year, the summer may be the only time you'll have to really focus on this important task. Keep in mind that the application timeline is rapidly approaching at that point (as early as November of your senior year for some schools).

How an Essay Can Tip the Scales in Your Favor

Although sentiments vary regarding what an essay can do in terms of optimizing an applicant's chances for acceptance (or, conversely, detracting from an applicant's candidacy), there were some common themes among admissions experts.

Gil Villanueva (Brandeis) noted that "a poorly written essay and/or an inappropriate topic can and will affect the admission decision. Many selective institutions often choose from many academically qualified candidates. As a general rule, the selectivity index of an institution denotes the level of subjectivity in their admissions selection process. An exceptional essay, on the other hand, may prompt an admissions officer to give an applicant a second look."

Richard Zeiser, the Dean of Admission at the University of Hartford, cited several instances in his experience where applicants weakened their presentation (and resulting chances of admission) through submission of essays that were poorly written, not proofread, and contained egregious errors (psychology spelled wrong for a prospective psych major; the name of a different university plugged into what was apparently a generic essay; and blatant errors in punctuation, grammar, and syntax). He added that with these obvious problems, an admissions reader becomes so distracted by the errors while reading the essay "that it colors the way the content is interpreted." The net result? "It reflects poorly on the applicant."

Eric Simonelli (University of Rhode Island) commented that "an essay can help a student more than it can hurt one. If a student had been involved with a unique circumstance or situation that has affected his or her performance in the classroom and has explained this effectively in the essay, we will take those circumstances into consideration before making a decision. However, when evaluating a student's file here at URI, the most important information is a student's rank in class, overall weighted GPA, competitive level of the high school (what percentage of students attend four-year universities), and standardized test scores. However, the power of the essay lies in the hands of the student."

Douglas Christiansen, Ph.D., Associate Provost for Enrollment and Dean of Admissions at Vanderbilt University, stated that "a well-crafted, heartfelt, and authentic essay can make a difference in whether a student is admitted or denied. With all other things being equal, yes, [the essay] absolutely can matter."

Distinguish Yourself in Your Essay—But Be Authentic

According to Chris Muñoz, Vice President for Enrollment, Rice University, "Applicants can write their essays in such a way that the reader senses

© JIST Works

authenticity. I think that this is very important, especially if you are looking at ways of distinguishing strong candidates as in the case of the most highly selective universities like Rice. A number of students that are put on the wait list and some that are eventually denied admission (especially those on wait lists) statistically presented top GPAs and test scores. A very high proportion of the students that apply to Rice have 4.0 GPAs, have AP/Honors courses, and, at Rice, among matriculants, this last year's mean SAT scores were over 1400 (verbal and math). Sometimes, however, even candidates with strong quantitative applications can fail to distinguish themselves as individuals. The essay, along with letters of recommendation, can play a stronger role or bigger role in the decision."

Vince Cuseo (Occidental) had this to say about the weight of the application essay in decision making about an applicant's candidacy: "It depends upon the individual application. It's less reliable than many of the other elements of the application, but it may matter more or less depending on the competitiveness of the other parts of the application. For instance, if grades, scores, extracurriculars, and recommendations place a student 'on the bubble,' the essay may be the deciding factor." He also added that "the more selective the college, the more the institution must discriminate among a rarefied set of applicants with comparably impressive statistics. Qualitative measures then take on more of a role, such as the essay."

Don Bishop (Creighton) concurs that a strong application (from the standpoint of transcript and SAT scores) can be hurt by a mediocre essay and shares the following:

If a student has a poorly written essay or one that shows simplistic thinking, yet they have higher academic statistics, we tend to grade that student down considerably. There are too many good applicants with strong academic records. So a disappointing essay that is sloppy or simplistic can take a student from the realm of likely admit to a deny decision. You wonder if the student is truly interested in you and/or if the student is as sharp as their overall record.

It is not unusual to see an applicant with higher test scores than grades and a below-average essay effort. They are chronic underachievers and these students need to learn that a high test score is about number three or four on our list of priorities. Number one is sustained effort and wisdom obtained through caring about your work and getting better. The poor essay further documents the rift between their high scores and lower performance and is a compelling reason to aggressively turn these students down and not have them take a spot away from a hardworking student who will make better use of the educational opportunity at the college.

A student with an impressive essay that has lower test scores but high grades can gain ground with a thoughtful and articulate essay. It gives further evidence that the student is much better than their test scores and more like their daily effort in school.

Students with lower academics and a brilliant essay are suspected of having the essay developed for them. You simply cannot talk your way or write your way into a selective college. Your actions over the past several years are more important than a well-written essay. You cannot charm your way in when you have not done what others have done in the classroom.

Jeanne Jenkins (Rensselaer) adds, "No one denies a student with anything but great reluctance. We look for reasons *to* admit someone. Those students who are not accepted should keep in mind that it may not be that they are lacking something; rather, someone else might have just that one extra thing that tips the balance in their favor. College admissions, in general, is not about denying people—it's always about trying to find the right students."

Key Points: Chapter 1

- Because college admissions has become so competitive, concentrating on producing the best possible essay is one of the key ways to help your candidacy for admission.

- The summer following your junior year in high school is the optimal time to capture your essay ideas and begin to shape the content. Be authentic and tell *your story.*

- It is important to understand how your achievement fits in with the profile of typical students at the school of your choice—from where your SAT or ACT scores fall on the spectrum of admitted students to seeing where your GPA ranks. Schedule those final tests before beginning your senior year if you need one more round of test scores to boost your results.

- Pay close attention to the types of admission offered by the colleges of your choice—and if you're thinking of applying Early Decision or Early Action, be sure to have everything in order by October.

© JIST Works

Chapter 2

Advice from the Admission Pros: Selecting a Topic, Style, and Approach

A s noted in the Introduction, this book provides essential advice to high school juniors, seniors, and their parents/advisors gleaned from the expert opinion of veteran admissions professionals at respected universities around the country as well as the actual experiences of current college students. This chapter and the next provide essay-writing recommendations and strategies direct from the decision makers. In this chapter, you'll find specific recommendations from admissions experts along with many examples of what works (and what does not) when developing your application essay.

Quick Take-Away: What Your Essay Needs to Do

- **Be authentic.** You must be yourself—don't try to present what you think someone else wants to read.
- **Show who you really are.** What makes you unique? What about you is special? (It often helps to think of how others whose opinions you respect describe you.) What separates you from everyone else who might have similar qualifications on paper?
- **Show some enthusiasm!** You are selling yourself. And you are selling a university admissions office on why you'd be a great asset to their particular school. Why should you be a member of the incoming class of 2012, for instance? What will you contribute? What do you absolutely, positively love about this school? Why is it the perfect fit for you?
- **Remember that the essay can make a big difference.** A carefully written essay can tip the scales positively in favor of a candidate whose application is on par in every other way with what a school is seeking—and help the candidate to stand out among a pool of similarly

qualified candidates. A poorly written essay can spell doom for candidates whose credentials put them squarely on a fence with other candidates vying for too few spaces and may be the one criterion that turns a possible yes into a definite no.

- **Create a compelling picture of you!** Your transcript says a lot about your academic performance—but it's one-dimensional. Likewise, your ACT or SAT scores show something of your inherent strengths (and about how well you perform on a standardized test). Your letters of recommendation should provide keen insights into who you are. But your essay is the one tool over which you have complete control to paint a picture that's accurate, real, and interesting.

Some General Advice

Many dozens of deans and directors of admission, vice presidents of enrollment, and senior-level admissions experts at universities and colleges across the United States were polled for their best-in-class advice about the college application essay. Those admissions professionals who agreed to be quoted and included in this book reflect a diverse range of institutions; their experience in the university admissions field exceeds 300 years collectively. Here, then, is the wisdom of an elite group of admissions professionals on the application essay and the admissions process in general.

Admissions Philosophy

Chris Muñoz, the Vice President for Enrollment at Rice University, shares the following philosophy with respect to admissions. A similar approach was echoed by many admissions experts.

History shows that no single gauge can adequately predict a student's preparedness for a successful career at Rice. For example, we are cautious in the use of standardized test scores to assess student preparedness and potential. An applicant's entire file is considered and each applicant is considered in competition with all other applicants. In making a decision to admit or award scholarships or financial aid, we are careful not to ascribe too much value to any single metric, such as rank in class, grade-point average, or the SAT/ACT.

© JIST Works

We use a broader perspective that includes, for example, such qualitative factors as the overall strength and competitive ranking of a student's prior institution, the rigor of his or her particular course of study, letters of recommendation, essays, responses to application questions, and (where required) auditions and portfolios. Taken together with a student's academic record and test scores, these kinds of additional factors provide a sound basis to begin assessing the applicant's potential on all levels.

Beyond indicators of academic competence, we look for other qualities among applicants such as creativity, motivation, artistic talent, and leadership potential. We believe that students who possess these attributes in combination with strong academic potential will contribute to, and benefit from, a more vibrant, diverse educational atmosphere. Through their contributions and interactions with others, students will enrich the educational experience of all faculty and students. These qualities are not revealed in numerical measurements, but are manifest in the breadth of interests and the balance of activities in their lives.

Be Authentic, Trust Yourself

From Douglas Christiansen, Ph.D., Associate Provost for Enrollment and Dean of Admissions at Vanderbilt University: "At the end of the day, we are trying to see if what the student is communicating to us is a fit for the type of student body we are trying to develop. First and foremost, students should not try to think of what it is we want. They should really talk in their own voices, expressing their authentic feelings on whatever the essay question is asking. Students need to remember that we know they are only 17—their ability to be a reflective writer at the magnitude of someone who is 50 or 60 with vastly different life experiences simply isn't there.

"With 21 years in higher education reading thousands of essays, I can say that the most authentic results come from students who tell us who they are, articulate their story clearly, and express their true feelings. They do much better in the whole process than [the student who presents] an essay that looks overly packaged, over-read, and has been scrutinized by 19 people. Of course it makes sense to have someone (an English teacher, for instance) read over the essay and offer ideas on how to polish it, that is part of the collaborative educational process."

Jeanne Jenkins, Director of Strategic Initiatives within the Admissions Office of Rensselaer Polytechnic Institute, provides useful insights into the admissions process within a technological university.

> *Very few people apply to a college like this who are not, on a fundamental level, absolutely qualified to do the work. But among academically qualified applicants, we are even more interested in students who can express themselves in writing. This is essential because, as a technology university, we expect that students interested in applying are going to have a strong interest and skills in science and mathematics. But writing skills are critical—successful engineers, management people, architects, and scientists must be good communicators with people who do not have their same backgrounds. Hence, we value the writing piece (the application essay) and while we do not pay a disproportionate amount of attention to it, it is viewed very carefully.*

Be Introspective and Express Yourself

Admissions experts consistently state that the best essays are introspective—providing that all-important peek into who the candidate really is and what he or she has to offer. It goes without saying (but so many essays would appear to ignore this cardinal rule) that the essay should be interesting, capturing the reader's attention. It doesn't necessarily have to be that the subject is so captivating; rather, your style in bringing the reader into your world is what is key. Is the writing engaging? Or is it ho-hum, recitational, and a recap of everything on the application and/or resume? Ideally, the essay will explore something not revealed elsewhere in the application. Perhaps it is a quiet but fascinating (to you) hobby into which you've poured hundreds of hours (over many years). Maybe it's a relationship with a special-needs student in a day camp that has been nurtured over the past few years. It might be that it is a relationship with a family elder (grandparent or great-aunt/great-uncle) that has allowed you to develop compassion in a different way while learning stories of heritage. Maybe it relates to special skills you've developed through a nonacademic interest: Has your competitive chess-playing ability translated into higher-level math skills?

© JIST Works

The Essay Is "the Fingerprint" of Each Individual

According to Jeanne Jenkins, Rensselaer Polytechnic Institute, "The essay can be equated with being a piece of DNA. With a highly selective university, such as RPI, the aggregate scores, GPA, transcripts, and so forth of dozens if not hundreds of students will provide exactly the same statistical picture. But only you (the student) are going to write your essay. It is the one distinguishing item in your application package; it serves as a fingerprint of every single individual."

Connect the Dots

Are there things reflected in your application materials that you can better illuminate through your essay? This can reveal either triumphant or difficult moments. If your performance during sophomore year really tanked, can you offer an explanation? Did you try to get involved in too many clubs and activities in addition to taking on two foreign languages and a part-time job in the spring—all leaving you with too little time to get the job done? If you 'righted the ship' during your junior year and have stayed on track ever since, this can be a good story to tell. Likewise, did your years of dance training translate into a performing role with a local musical stage production company that meant you had rehearsals and/or performances seven days a week—for three months (and maybe grades that dipped precipitously low for one semester)? Again, tell the story and share what the experience taught you.

Keep It Personal—But Not Embarrassingly So

You want to write about what is real to you and about you—not someone else you admire. You may have had an incredible coach, and it's fine to draw this into your essay. But the emphasis should be on how this coach helped shape you as an individual, helped you see things from a different perspective, or taught you to draw on new inner wells of strength you didn't know existed. If you share a story of collaborating with others on a major project (in school or perhaps within the community), this can be compelling. Just be certain that it is an event that carries great meaning about who you are as a person and that the story will allow you to share what role you played, how you felt, and what the results meant to you personally. Do be sure your topic is appropriate—and won't embarrass you, your family, or the reader.

Tips for Selecting the Best Essay Topic for You

Finding a topic to write about can be one of the most perplexing steps in the college admissions process. Many students think they haven't done something "important enough" to write about. Or they may worry that their special interest (such as a hobby, sport, or type of music) just won't engage an admissions dean. They think that their entry must be Pulitzer-worthy and worry that they simply won't stand out in a pool crowded with high-achieving applicants, all of whom they think are far more accomplished (and have written the equivalent of *War and Peace* to accompany their applications!).

Jeanne Jenkins (Rensselaer) states that "The hardest part of the essay is not writing it—but deciding on the topic and how you are going to approach it. What is your message going to be? Once you've figured that out, the essay pretty comfortably writes itself."

As you'll read here and throughout this book, colleges want to know the applicants as well as they possibly can from those few sheets of paper. They want to see a glimmer of the applicant's personality, of who they really are. They want to know what a student is passionate about; where he or she draws his greatest energy. If there's a link to the institution and higher learning, fine—but that's not the be-all and end-all of the process.

Write What You Know

Whether you ascribe to the old-school, "Write what you know," or the more contemporary version, "Write what you want to know," chances are you've heard these expressions from more than one teacher or counselor. With the college essay-writing project, it makes sense to consider what you know and feel energy or emotion about before deciding on the essay topic. Remember that the topic does not have to be about an issue of global importance. Many students make the mistake of tackling major social issues and fall short of revealing much about themselves. If you are actively involved in Habitat for Humanity, for instance, and it has made a real difference in your life (for instance, you have changed what you want to study in college from being an illustrator to learning more about public administration and how you can impact program development), talk about the moment when it became clear to you that you could see yourself making a difference. But don't just write about a good cause for its own sake.

© JIST Works

You need to show how this has helped you become the person you are today—or the one you wish to become.

Consider one aspect of your background that may show up briefly on your transcript and delve into the behind-the-scenes story for your essay. For example, if you participate in a WISE (Wise Individualized Senior Experience) program that your high school offers seniors, describe how you selected your topic, talk about what you are passionate about, and share the story of something you learned, something that surprised you (perhaps about yourself), or something that was emotionally touching.

Vince Cuseo, Dean of Admission, Occidental College, offers some key insights into selection of an essay topic. "The ubiquitous summer volunteer experience in *(name a foreign country)* is a hackneyed topic. Some topics just make it more challenging to communicate something that defines who you are and in a manner that pulsates with personality. But I really believe any topic is fair game if it reveals something meaningful about you. So it's not the topic itself, but the *approach* to the topic that matters."

Be Careful with Tragic Subjects

Doug Christiansen (Vanderbilt) recommends students use caution when writing about a very tragic story or extreme experience. "If the 'extreme' experience is real, provided an opportunity for reflection, and means something to the student, then this can be very appropriate. But if the subject selected has the 'appearance' of a life-shaping experience but in fact did not alter one's perspective or thought, then it might be construed as a technique being used in the essay to garner attention. The most important thing is for a student to articulate particular thoughts or feelings about their topic and express clearly what it means (or meant) to them. It can be very basic; sometimes the simplest things can have the greatest impacts in life."

Jean Jordan, Interim Dean of Admission, Emory University, comments that "students don't have to have had some horrific illness or injury—and their families can be intact—in order to write a great essay. I try to steer students away from some of the topics that colleges get frequently [lots of mission trips], unless it is something that has really impacted their lives significantly upon their return home. Stories can be on a very local level—such as when a student starts some kind of volunteer organization in their own hometown."

Questions to Ask Yourself

Don Bishop, Associate Vice President for Enrollment Management, Creighton University, said, "Whatever topic you choose, it should relate to the admissions committee that you have both a sharp mind—that thinks reflectively (you learn and gain wisdom from thinking)—and character with an active heart—that creates an active effort to make a difference in something you care about." He offered some specific questions to ask yourself:

Discuss a specific involvement you experienced and state

- Why did you do this?
- How did doing this demonstrate something about your personality and personal values?
- What did you do to accomplish the effort?
- Did you do anything creative or challenging to create the result?
- What happened to others as a result of your actions?
- Did you make a difference? What did you gain from the experience?
- What new things did you learn about yourself and about others?
- What wisdom did you achieve from this activity?

After telling this story, you should then discuss the following:

- How will your four years at this college allow you to build on this important experience?
- What will you do at this college based on the new wisdom you gained from this activity?
- What will you do after the college years as it relates to the topic you discussed in your essay?

Use the Essay to Clarify Your Application

Gil Villanueva, Dean of Admissions, Brandeis University, pointed out that "there is added value to writing about topics that may not be reflected elsewhere in the application. Also, the essay provides the ideal avenue for an applicant to address a potentially controversial or unclear aspect of their application." Some admissions experts suggest that students with less than stellar SAT/ACT scores or spotty transcripts (occasional Cs and Ds) use the essay to honestly and succinctly explain their stories.

Be Authentic

Chris Muñoz (Rice) was very clear that students not "write an essay based on some 'best guess' that the topic is what a university may be interested in based on their profile." For instance, he notes that in the area of service leadership—a topic frequently written about—if the experience is not truly authentic enough, deep enough, it may not help the candidate's application. Mr. Muñoz does share the sentiment, "write about what you know best and let that stand for you. Again, demonstrate you know something about the institution to which you are applying—convey authenticity."

Hints on Approaching Your Essay

The admissions professionals interviewed for this book had a variety of opinions on the best approaches for your essay.

- **Appeal to the admissions officer's investigational side.** "Essays that cause readers to use their senses are particularly fun. Admission officers are natural investigators, so we enjoy learning about an applicant's outlook on life, family background, or meaningful experience. For the most part, strong students tend to present good essays. The rare instances where we detect disparities between the student's essay and academic performance and on standardized testing seem to occur when there are other educational or personal issues of which we need to be aware." (Gil Villanueva, Brandeis)

No Cookie-Cutter Approaches

Vince Cuseo, Dean of Admission, Occidental College, had some hints about differentiating your essay from the others. "The best essays are the ones with soul. They're real. They're more conversational than calculated. And they feel as if no one could have authored them other than the writer. There is nothing cookie-cutter about them."

- **Point out problems and how you solved them.** "It is very effective for students to point out problems in their school or community and then talk about how they approached solving these problems—what they did that made their school or community better. Why did they think that it was important and what did they learn from that experience? How will that experience translate into action during their college years and then after college?" (Don Bishop, Creighton)

- **Show your methodical or creative side.** "Interestingly, science applicants often appear to compose essays in a methodical manner. There are times when the creative-writing or English major can be spotted easily for they, as a group, tend to write freely, exhibiting no inhibitions. On the whole, for highly selective schools, the essay can be an excellent indicator of the student's ability to do the work on the collegiate level." (Gil Villanueva, Brandeis)

Avoid Procrastinating—and Do Revisit the Next Day

Paul Marthers, Dean of Admission, Reed College, has some savvy advice about getting started early on essays. "Procrastination often leads to sloppiness or ill-conceived attempts at humor (such as the essay that had a string of expletives in the opening sentence or the handwritten essay about Elvis, my hero). Both essays probably wouldn't have passed the let-it-steep-then-revisit-it-before-sending test."

- **Turn a mundane topic into something very interesting.** "When I worked at Vassar in the mid-80s, I read an essay on the unremarkable topic of getting a haircut that became a big hit around the office. The young man, who was admitted, took a self-deprecatingly humorous approach, much like the style that has since made David Sedaris famous." (Paul Marthers, Reed)

- **Do something extraordinarily creative.** "The most unique thing a student ever did was to actually take the Emory University song and then change the lyrics to tell the story of why he should be admitted. The time and effort that went into researching the school song, making the story authentic, and telling why he should be accepted and what he would do once on campus truly stood out." (Jean Jordan, Emory)

- **Discuss your passion for a field of study.** "If students have a particular passion for a field of study, they should discuss that field and tell us why they have passion for it and also try to convince us they are talented in that field. If the essay is open-ended, one particular approach is for a student to write a recommendation or cover letter for themselves for a position they someday hope to reach. This essay could include not only what they have already accomplished, but also what they wish to accomplish during college and soon after college." (Don Bishop, Creighton)

- **Ring a bell.** "The best essays are those that are genuine and have a special quality about them—whether it's humor, poignancy, or something else that I would certainly like to believe cannot be contrived. The well-written essay rings a bell, clearly and simply." (Jeanne Jenkins, Rensselaer)

© JIST Works

Be Your Own Creative Self

Don Bishop, Associate Vice President for Enrollment Management, Creighton University, has some words of wisdom about creativity. "If a college stresses the value of being creative or invites you to consider submitting an essay that demonstrates your creativity—think about how you are creative and use something that fits your sense of creativity—don't copy something from another person that you think was creative in a general sense. Sum up whatever you can from your own experience and be as creative as you can be—don't compare that with some of the more interesting and admittedly entertaining 'stunt' creative essays that you see on the Internet.

"Believe me, the college has seen too many copies of these 'creative essays' as submissions by students pretending these to be their authentic work. When we see such copies, those students are absolutely discounted and placed well below those who at least tried to be themselves."

Eric Simonelli's (Admission Advisor, University of Rhode Island) advice also emphasizes the authentic: "It is always nice when a student writes about a person or experience that has influenced them in a positive way (this might be a family experience, a teacher, a coach, a situation, or a memory). My favorite essays are those that are touching and demonstrate to me that the individual can positively affect URI—that they can make a difference on campus."

The Bottom Line

Richard Zeiser, Dean of Admission, University of Hartford, presents the ultimate information he wants to see in an essay: "Tell us why you think that this would be a place that would be a good institution that will help bring out your talents or help you to develop skills and knowledge that will help you get where you want to go."

The Do's and the Don'ts

The following section contains helpful recommendations from many of the admissions deans and experts featured throughout this book. Remember: These are the ultimate "decision makers," the people reading the thousands of applications (and essays) crossing their desks each year. Their opinions are valuable to the savvy student trying to best approach the task of writing an authentic application essay. You'll also find interspersed among these do's and don'ts anecdotal advice from a variety of additional sources.

The Do's

Starting with the *do's*, you'll find a number of good suggestions to use in developing your application essay.

- **Do make sure that you are genuine and can explain who you are as a person that can separate you from someone else.** Answer these two questions in writing the essay:

  1. What makes me different from the next person applying to this school?
  2. How can I show the school what I can bring to the table that is not on my transcript? (Eric Simonelli, University of Rhode Island)

- **Do use your voice.** Do not pretend to be anyone else. Admission officers are interested in learning about *you*. We are not particularly interested in a book report. Your essay allows your application to come alive. (Gil Villanueva, Brandeis)

- **Do know yourself.** This is in a similar vein as using your own voice. Effective essays are rooted in self-reflection. Students with an accurate and deep understanding of their interests and passions are best positioned to author an engaging essay. This isn't easy: We understand that. Introspection doesn't come naturally to 17-year-olds, particularly in an era that rewards busy-ness over self-reflection. So carve out some time to just plain think. Good writing mirrors good thinking. What matters most to you? What energizes you? What makes you, *you* and no one else? Your essay should be an authentic representation of your distinctiveness. (Vince Cuseo, Occidental)

- **Do your research.** If you're talking about pursuit of engineering studies toward an eventual career in civil engineering, make sure the college you're applying to offers (a) an engineering program to start with and/or (b) a civil engineering major.

- **Do give consideration to writing in the third person.** It can be an effective strategy. (Jeanne Jenkins, Rensselaer)

- **Do remember that whatever the selected topic, vivid, confident, concise writing is always impressive.** (Paul Marthers, Reed)

- **Do tell the admissions committee about one or two activities that led you to a greater understanding of yourself and others around you.** Tell them why you did that activity, what you learned from that

© JIST Works

activity, and how your future actions will be influenced by this greater awareness. If at all possible, connect that awareness with what you plan to do at their college. Colleges are looking for interesting thinkers who will contribute to the campus community, to the community after college, and also to a profession. If the applicant has a special talent or passion for something that is valued at the college—an academic strength, performing arts, sports, or leadership/service—this will be important to incorporate into the essay. The essay should be descriptive of your personality—what defines you and what drives you, but it also needs to tell the reader why their college will benefit from your enrollment. With respect to writing style, be yourself, but be your most impressive, expressive self. (Don Bishop, Creighton)

- **Do be creative and strive for some variety in the appearance of your writing.** Exceptionally long blocks of narrative text will not be as enticing to the reader as a variety of mixed-length paragraphs. If there is a particular thesis statement or sentence that really sums things up nicely in your essay, it might stand nicely on its own—and will certainly garner the reader's attention.

- **Do showcase your talent.** Be yourself and select a topic that you feel confident writing about. (Jean Jordan, Emory)

- **Do tell the reader what about the college especially interests you—** why it made your list and, especially if it's truly your first choice, why. Admission deans want to know honestly why you believe you are the right fit for the school and what about the particular combination of campus/academics/other key factors resonated with you. You'll read in chapter 4 an essay designed for the specific purpose of getting a college to reject the applicant (very unusual, but it will make sense when you read the back story).

- **Do remember that the best essays** "are the ones that clearly represent something from the heart or something that is very certainly an aspect of the student's character, perspective, or outlook. This can't be manufactured." (Jeanne Jenkins, Rensselaer)

- **Do write in an active voice—with lots of action words to tell your story.** It's not a bedtime story, as several essay readers pointed out. You want to hold the reader's attention and stand out from among a pile of hundreds (and even thousands) of essays.

- **Do use a sense of humor, with some restraint.** The essay is not a comedy piece, but admissions officers enjoy and are impressed with the appropriate use of humor, which indicates wit. For example, an applicant from a small city in Montana was trying to impress the admissions committee that coming from a non-urban area meant they had a unique perspective that would add to our campus community of largely suburban and urban students. In their essay, one of the six paragraphs they wrote was dedicated to the town's exuberance when a McDonald's was built and opened in their city. They described with sarcasm how the city had a parade for the event... "it was as if the big brains at McDonald's had looked down from the clouds and seen our little town and blessed it as a thriving little city—worthy of Big Macs, fries and Happy Meals. The opening of McDonald's in the minds of residents ratified our town and all of us as worthy citizens of the United States. After that day no one from our town considered themselves as isolated from the world." The student made it clear that this was mockingly stated. (Don Bishop, Creighton)

- **Do tell the story—your story.** No matter how interesting a topic you have researched might be to share, it won't be about you. You want to tell the admissions committee enough so that they know what truly distinguishes you from other candidates.

- **Do be patient.** Good writing takes several drafts. Be specific and descriptive. (Vince Cuseo, Occidental)

- **Do proofread and also vary your words.** Use words you have used but use your best vocabulary. Come up with a second word to describe your feelings and thoughts. You cannot repeat the same word over and over without losing some of its impact. As an example: "...I am really very interested in community service....very interested in helping others...very interested in making a difference in the lives of others" can be restated in an essay as follows: "I am passionate about community service...deeply committed to helping others...dedicated to making a difference in the lives of others." (Don Bishop, Creighton)

- **Do set it aside.** If time allows, it is good to not look at your essay for a few days after you think you've completed it. When you come back to the essay with fresh eyes, you'll see things from a new perspective and quickly be able to pick out any problem areas. Only after you've

© JIST Works

done this a few times and are feeling you have produced your absolute best work should you then share it with a trusted reader (a parent, teacher, or counselor) for feedback.

The Don'ts

The following list covers a broad range of topics *most* students are advised to steer clear of in selecting their essay topic. This draws on information shared by college admissions officers as well as high school guidance counselors.

The Number-One Don't: Don't Forget to Proof It!

The number one don't from virtually every admissions expert is this: Don't forget to carefully proofread your essay. The types of errors to watch for include the following:

- Grammatical problems
- Spelling errors
- Syntax issues
- Incorrect punctuation
- Using the wrong university name (in other words, taking a template essay and forgetting to edit it)
- Overuse of certain words (such as *really* and *very*)

Some of the obvious don'ts include the following:

- Don't plagiarize.

- Don't have someone else write your essay.

- Don't fabricate information.

- Don't mimic exactly what appears on the college's Web site or in the viewbook—be original.

- Don't provide a laundry list of activities and awards in the essay without giving any depth to their importance and relevance; instead, focus on one or two of the most important and share what you learned and why it was important.

- Avoid the cliché and trite.

- Don't select a topic you are unfamiliar with or uncomfortable discussing.

© JIST Works

- Be careful with the trip to a foreign land "that transformed you" essay; it has been done many, many times before and often ends up inadvertently reinforcing negative stereotypes about applicants from economically privileged backgrounds.

- Know your audience; consider how the reader will react to your topic and your method of delivery.

The following are specific recommendations from admissions experts along with additional anecdotal advice. These are grouped into three categories: "Topic," "Approach," and "Style" (writing and mechanics).

Topic Don'ts

Notes Don Bishop (Creighton), "Many of these topics are usually ineffective for application essays...they are not unique to you and they show a certain level of either ordinary thinking or immaturity."

- **Avoid sports stories.** Telling the committee how you made or did not make the key play in an athletic competition or season...sports is just not going to be very important to the admissions committee. They are more concerned and interested with your life as a student in their classrooms and your citizenship in their residential campus. (Don Bishop, Creighton)

- **Don't make yourself appear self-involved.** Try to avoid writing about trips to Europe that lend themselves to listing where you went and how surprised you were that your inability to speak any other language made people in other countries feel Americans are self-involved and detached from a global awareness—unless you came back, took more foreign-language courses, and you intend to do a study abroad and major in international affairs or international business. (Don Bishop, Creighton)

The Essay **Must** *Be Your Own Original Work*

From Paul Marthers, Dean of Admission, Reed College: Don't even think of copying someone else's essay or getting one off the Internet. Such behavior is unethical, and if you are caught your application will be rejected or your admission will be revoked after the fact.

- **Don't name-drop.** Nearly every expert interviewed for this book said it really doesn't make a difference if your uncle's employer's first cousin is a senator who attended the same school.

- **Don't call attention to negatives.** Avoid dwelling on your lower-than-you-wanted SAT or ACT test scores. (Don Bishop, Creighton)

- **Don't focus on others.** Avoid talking about how smart everyone else is in your family. If you are the lowest talent in the family, it does not matter to us that your parents went to a top college or that your brother or sister is enrolled at an elite university. This is about you, not them. Focusing your comments on others demonstrates a lack of confidence in yourself. (Don Bishop, Creighton)

- **Don't pick an inappropriate subject or use sarcasm.** Be especially careful if tackling a subject that could be considered inappropriate (underage alcohol consumption, drug use). Be equally cautious using humor or sarcasm to tell your story, especially if these techniques are affected and not natural. While carefully done these approaches can be effective, there is probably a greater risk that these approaches will falter.

- **Don't write about dead relatives or friends.** Teenagers all have experienced death through a friend or relative. This is just not a unique enough experience—no matter how traumatic it was for you, it was for all of us…we have all been there and done that. If you have lost a parent or close sibling you can comment on this within a grander message in your essay, but it should not be the lone message—that you survived that ordeal. You need to state how that will affect your future actions and make you a more compelling person than others. (Don Bishop, Creighton)

Be Wary of Championship Stories

Approach championship and victory stories with caution. Winning the state baseball championship is undoubtedly a high point in your life at this point—but it's a story admissions officers have read way too many times already. Now, if you overcame an unusual circumstance to participate, there might be something noteworthy in the story you could tell. Likewise, a story of defeat is probably not a good topic to address. However, if there was an opportunity to really learn something about yourself that appears life-changing and has altered your future course, that could be an interesting story.

- **Don't use a list format.** Don't write in your essay a simple string of comments that basically list what activities you did and awards you received in high school. That is not an essay. (Don Bishop, Creighton)

- **Don't parrot the marketing material.** Avoid stating the primary reasons you want to go to a college by restating the statements they wrote in their viewbook and Web site. Restating to the admissions committee the words of their marketing team that wrote all those platitudes in their viewbook and Web site will not endear you to the admissions team. It will appear that you just copied their own material and gave it back to them with little effort on your part for self-reflection. (Don Bishop, Creighton)

Approach Don'ts

- **Don't forget to take the audience into account.** Remember to whom you are writing. Sometimes applicants extend lengthy essays or appear to be trying to use too many SAT words. (Gil Villanueva, Brandeis)

- **Don't make the mistake of writing one essay (even if it's a good one) and using it for all situations.** Really consider your audience carefully, the points you are wishing to make, and the approach you are using. (And if you do use cut-and-paste, be doubly sure to check for the college's name in the essay so that you are not sending out the wrong essay.)

- **Don't procrastinate and put off the essay until a week or less from the deadline.** Good writing needs time to steep or coagulate. Write a draft, put it aside, reread it when you have some perspective. Are you excited about it? Does a trusted adviser like it? (Paul Marthers, Reed)

- **Don't just dash it off.** Except for a situation where you absolutely must have the essay together in just an hour or two, don't think that you can write the essay, proofread it once, and be done with it. As any writer will tell you, editing (and proofreading) a document is as important as writing it. Go back many times (preferably not on the same day as you wrote it). Using a fresh perspective will help you to catch errors that the eye automatically fills in. Try to see whether each sentence really moves the story along and adds meaning. Does it flow smoothly? Is the writing crisp and clear? Is anything muddled or confusing? Really be critical (in a positive way) of your original work. Remember that virtually every book you read (including textbooks, this book, and your favorite work of fiction) is not as the author initially wrote it in the first draft. In most cases, the material has been edited, reviewed, revised, and reshaped a number of times.

© JIST Works

- **Don't let 'too many cooks spoil the stew.'** The essay will lose its personal voice if too many others offer advice on how to tweak it. (Vince Cuseo, Occidental)

- **Don't be overly coached in your essay-writing.** With the input of too many well-meaning people, the essay can turn into something that really isn't your work—and is not truly genuine. (Jeanne Jenkins, Rensselaer)

Style Don'ts

- **Don't use vocabulary that you never use.** Readers can tell if you are comfortable with your words and you may also misuse a word and convey an unintended meaning. If your vocabulary happens to be exceptional, this will show on your test scores and transcript; resist the urge to show off in your essay. Also delete every single "very" and "really." If you are "very interested," think about using a word like "intrigued." If you are "really committed," think about using a word like "passionate" or "dedicated." It is time for you to use more descriptive, exact words and not rely on how you chat informally among your friends. (Don Bishop, Creighton)

Stay Away from Satire

From Jean Jordan, Interim Dean of Admission, Emory University: "Don't write in a satirical style (unless you are extremely accomplished). Several years ago, a student attempted to use satire in tackling the subject of homosexuality for an application submitted to a very liberal college with a highly open and inclusive environment. The essay fell completely flat, on top of which the staff was mortified and found the satire to be inappropriate and offensive."

- **Don't be too self-serving.** While you may be hoping to get the best education possible by attending a particular school—so that you can have a top-paying job on Wall Street, that motivation is likely to fall flat in an essay.

- **Don't ramble.** Don't go on and on in a boring manner about something that will have little meaning to anyone else. Get to the point—and really focus on the message you are trying to impart (what you learned, what it meant to you, how you changed, and so forth).

- **Don't set out to write an essay that is cute or clever.** It will look contrived. Although you may be able to strike an interesting tone that is perceived as endearing or clever, you don't want to start with that as your mission.

- **Don't be too formal in your writing style.** While it's important to have excellent spelling, punctuation, and syntax (to the degree of your abilities—with modest editing help from a trusted resource), the essay should not be a formal dissertation. There should be a sense of conveying who you are, one-to-one, with the reader. This piece of writing should leave the reader with a better sense of who you really are and how you think. Some experts suggest making the essay almost conversational in style.

- **Don't go significantly under or over the word or page length requirements for the essay.** While we don't hold students exactly to a word count, it becomes a hardship if the essay is extremely long. By the same token, if the essay is too short, it indicates a lack of thought and perhaps even a lack of interest in the university. (Jean Jordan, Emory)

- **Don't ignore directions**—and don't write an essay that is too long or too short. It's important to stay within the guidelines that the college or university has established. (Eric Simonelli, University of Rhode Island)

- **Don't tell too complicated a story**—or use too many creative devices (such as excessive dialogue, flashbacks, fade-ins, asides, and the like).

- **Don't use abbreviations that you have learned to use in text messaging or e-mails** (no OMG or ROFL allowed). These are not acceptable in written essays or personal statements. Obviously, slang and curse words are unacceptable as well. (Don Bishop, Creighton)

You'll find additional expertise from the admission experts in chapter 3, where they share their favorite essays and vignettes and discuss trends in admission. There is also good information about feedback to students, plus the expert opinion on seeking professional help with writing application essays.

© JIST Works

Key Points: Chapter 2

- Selecting the essay topic that is right for you is essential. Give yourself enough time to experiment with different ideas to find the one topic that really resonates with you and that you can feel excited about.

- Your style of writing should be natural and comfortable. Don't try to use a style you've never tried before. Keep it authentic and real—but convey a sense of your personality.

- Use the language you would use in writing a high school paper; don't try for special effects in determining your writing approach. Keep the SAT words to a minimum—and always proofread carefully.

Chapter 3

More Advice from the Admission Pros: Assistance, Feedback, Examples, and Trends

The valuable expertise provided by the admission professionals in chapter 2 with regard to your essay topic, style, and approach continues in this chapter. You'll learn their recommendations about whether you should have assistance with writing your resume (and the most appropriate methods), the types of feedback you're likely to receive about your essay, some excellent examples of what *not to do* as well as what can work—in your essay, and key admission trends.

Should You Seek Professional Help with Your Essay?

The answer from most admissions experts is that this should not be necessary. It is never appropriate to hire someone to write the essay, nor should someone else tell you what you should write about. But teachers, guidance counselors, and parents can provide guidance in terms of helping you to focus on drawing out your true story.

Advice for Parents Who Want to Help

There are ways of tapping assistance that can and do make sense for many students. Parents, especially, are in a great position to help a student focus on a particular topic—not by saying, "Sarah, you should write about x-y-z." Instead, this counsel would best take the form of question-and-answer: "Sarah, as you think of the past three years in high school, what stands out in your mind as the most surprising learning experience you have had?" "If you were given an opportunity to relive one day in your life, what day would you pick and why?" Questions like these can help a student start thinking along creative lines and foster the introspective thinking critical to writing a quality essay.

But probably the top form of assistance an interested adult can provide is proofreading. Additional ideas follow.

Creighton University's Associate Vice President for Enrollment Management, Don Bishop, discussed this topic at length:

Private consultants or high school counselors can review the student's first draft of their essay and give them opinions on what they have stated. These adults should not rewrite any part of the essay. I think it is important for the student to ask an adult whether their essay first-draft effort truly captures their essence as a person and their interest and match with a particular college. The adults often can tell a student that they have understated or oversold themselves. An adult who knows the student may also be able to reduce their anxiety about the essay by telling them a lot of the essay is good but certain parts are underwritten and underdeveloped—that the student needs to clarify a point and make the point more personal. Many students have never been trained on how to write essays. They have been trained to write reports. The adult can also reinforce the good sections of the essay and reaffirm to the student they are on the right path.

Having an adult give the student feedback can be an excellent learning moment for the student. In this way the essay may be one of the best learning opportunities for the student in the entire college admissions process.

The adult can give examples of topics but should not supply the topic for the essay. The adult can review with the student the list of topics being considered by the student and give the student their opinion on which topic may best reveal the true personality of the student.

The adult can review the final essay draft for basic grammar but should not rewrite the piece for the student. They can point out misspellings and grammatical errors and ask the student to fix them. I am always in favor of the student learning how to write properly. Writing their college essay is an intense moment in their life—they will often remember the corrections and this will improve their writing over the long term.

© JIST Works

To these universal points, the following comments were also offered:

- "We seek transparence. It's a vanishing commodity on both sides of the college-search equation—colleges and students are most interested in putting their best feet forward. But this doesn't mean it's not sought after. Frankly, the essay is the one part of an application that's easily manipulated. An unpolished writer can have his or her essay buffed by others, perhaps to the point where it has a sheen that's not reflective of the student's actual writing skill. Professional help is inappropriate and unnecessary." (Vince Cuseo, Occidental)

Take the Time to Be Introspective

Jeanne Jenkins, Director, Strategic Initiatives, Admissions Office, Rensselaer Polytechnic Institute, had this to say: "Rather than 'coach' students, I wish people would encourage students by telling them to be thoughtful and introspective. They should give themselves time to 'kick things around' in their heads before beginning to write."

- "Admission officers do not expect college-level work. We wish to learn if you can effectively convey your thought or message. If professional help is deemed necessary, then be sure to use your own voice, your own words, and your own ideas. In other words, you need to write the essay. In addition, admission officers find the best form of help comes from parents and teachers." (Gil Villanueva, Brandeis)

- "Use those people who are going to be your supporters and advocates in the college admission process. They can be your parents or your high school guidance counselors, but it's important to have open, honest conversations with them concerning what your ideas about college are. Try to make the process fun rather than something so stressful." (Jean Jordan, Emory)

More students get outside assistance today on their essays, ranging from private college consultants to Web sites that sell essays. Colleges are vigilant about essays that don't match up with the student's record and are able to often discount manufactured essays that are not truly developed by the student.

Do Colleges Ever Provide Students with Feedback About Their Essays?

It depends entirely on the school. From informal sampling, it appears as though 75 percent of schools do *not* provide any type of feedback relative to the essay. The 25 percent of institutions that do offer their applicants feedback specific to the essay do it only for accepted students. Here are a few thoughts from admissions experts:

- "Yes, we will e-mail a student if the essay is particularly moving—but only those students whom we think will merit admission! It would be cruel to applaud a student's essay in February and then deny them in late March." (Vince Cuseo, Occidental)

Effective Essays Bring Applications to Life

From Gil Villanueva, Dean of Admissions, Brandeis University: "The Committee on Admissions at Brandeis University carefully reads each and every application. We take special interest in reading essays, as they animate the many applications we receive. We are in the fortunate position to tell admitted applicants how much we enjoyed their work."

- "At Reed, we try to give candid, honest feedback when asked about an essay or some other part of the application. There have been times when we have asked applicants to explain why an essay looked similar to newspaper articles available on the Internet, for example. Our candid feedback is limited, of course, by what our legal counsel tells us is prudent." (Paul Marthers, Reed)

- "Yes, we will comment on a super-star essay. We usually attach a handwritten note, but, of course, only if the student is admissible." (Eric Simonelli, University of Rhode Island)

A number of universities commented that they do not provide feedback or subjective assessments about student performance in interviews or about student essays. The common refrain: "There is simply too much exposure of having these comments challenged or taken out of context."

© JIST Works

Strange, Curious, Provocative, Mediocre, and Winning Essays

Without exception, admissions deans all have stories about the funniest, most ridiculous, and most effective essays they have seen in their careers. Sometimes what is remembered is exceptional—but for the wrong reasons. Other times, an essay will stand out—and stand the test of time, being recalled for its value many years later. This section of the chapter shares some stories of inspiration—things you may want to consider doing and avoiding.

A Life-Changing Experience

Consider the following story shared by Jeanne Jenkins, Director, Strategic Initiatives, Admissions Office, Rensselaer Polytechnic Institute:

One of the most interesting essays I've read over the years was one from a young man who opted to write about community service. He was very honest and said that it was a requirement to get into the National Honor Society, but added that he really didn't want to go out and help people. Boxed into a corner with a looming deadline, he had to come up with something—so he selected the Special Olympics on the basis that it 'wouldn't take up much time' and 'wouldn't be hard.' This seemed a pretty good fit as he was an athlete himself.

What made this unusual was that after spending the requisite 30 hours with Special Olympics athletes to earn the community-service requirement, this young man discovered something much more than he had bargained for: He developed a special relationship with one of the athletes. In his essay, he spoke of the moments of clarity and personal revelation that hit him—that it wasn't about what he was giving to the Special Olympics program or to one athlete in particular; rather, it was what the athlete gave him. He came away from the experience 'blindsided' and amazed with the change in himself as a human being.

Standout Examples—Some Good and Some Bad

The following samples were provided by Don Bishop, Associate Vice President for Enrollment Management, Creighton University.

"Strangest Essay I've Ever Read [Out of More Than 55,000 in a 30-Year Career]"

A student wanted to go to a specialized art school but was told by his dad (an alumnus of the college where I was working) that if he got into his alma mater that he had to go and that the dad would not pay for any other college unless he was rejected at our college. The son explained this in the first paragraph of his essay, stating that as the only reason he had applied—that he was forced to apply.

His next paragraph discussed in detail why he felt another college was a better match for him with respect to his personal interests and academic focus—he was right. He also knew that his high achievement would normally gain admission to our highly selective school—he was also right about this.

Then his third paragraph was the most curious I have ever read—he requested we turn him down for admission and, to ensure we did, he then said something about our college that was crude and completely alienating. His final paragraph begged us to forgive his indelicate comment. He just needed to make that statement to ensure we understood how serious he was about us rejecting him. Needless to say, we accommodated his wishes.

This was a very sad story about a parent and student's lack of communication and team orientation—we blamed the dad, not the son, for this very sad state of affairs. We gave the son high marks for creativity!

Poor Writing

This essay is poorly written; there is a lack of focus, typos, and poor use of commas, and it uses simplistic, repetitive wording. The essay is also simplistic in thought with no depth. This individual seems like a dull thinker.

Based on the information that I myself have read, and on what my brother, who is presently attending [college name], has told me about it, I feel that I could receive the well-rounded education that I want there. My past is characterized by a great versatility in educational experiences, and I would like my future to follow the same pattern. My family has lived in Panama, Puerto Rico, Peru, and Venezuela, where I was able to benefit first-hand from the customs of another culture, as well as acquiring a foreign language. We then lived in Boston for several years, and are presently living in Sidney. My life in South America, the U.S., and Australia has been full of contrasts. I have had several jobs here in Sydney, have acquired a scholarship, several French awards, am an active participant in the

© JIST Works

school sports program, and have been on several committees during my years at high school. I believe that [college name] has much to offer me in the pursuit of further activities.

A Lack of Depth and Insight

This essay lists many things, but does not really convey much depth of thought—it accomplishes this only at a surface level. The writer appears to be a rather simplistic thinker who does not seem to reflect much on their core motivations. We really don't know why this person did all of these activities and what it means to them.

I have tried to be a leader in the activities which I have been involved. If I could not be an elected representative, then I tried to be a leader by example. Our Student Council felt that more Homecoming activities were in order. I was named Homecoming Dance Chairman. Against the forecasts of doom by the administration and many students, we organized the dance, worked to set it up, and it was a success. It was the first time in five years that it had been done, and it gave us a genuine feeling of accomplishment. I am also involved in CYO, having served as parish officer and now as an officer of the city's Deaneries Youth Council. CYO has meant very much to me and I believe in the work we do because it provides channels through which many young people can use their resources constructively to help others grow personally and also to help others. Hardly ever does a week go by that I am not involved in some CYO function, be it a swim meet, a baking contest, a Youth Week Pilgrimage, collecting clothes for the needy at Christmastime, or, most recently the election of our candidate to national CYO Federation President. I think my awards speak for themselves, and I am especially proud of the French award.

I worked for four years as a caddy and at several different restaurants. For my first three years of high school, I worked at the school for my tuition. This past summer, I worked for the U.S. Conservation Corps, a very rewarding experience which I would like to elaborate on if I had the space. I am presently employed at Bob's Standard Service Station, working 25 hours per week. I greatly desire a [college name] education for many reasons. The pre-med program is excellent. Aside from this I am attracted by the unique spirit of this great school, possibly the greatest of all private schools in America. I would like nothing better than to become part of your community. Thank you very much.

A Risk-Taker

This applicant took a risk in stating that too many students at our college were arrogant about their admission and enrollment at our college—though we also agreed with his assessment! He also demonstrated in his essay that he was a risk-taker during his high school career. We liked that.

In his senior year, this student was the editor of the college's newspaper. I wrote to him during his senior year and told him if he ever restated this essay for a graduate school or employer, to remember the next time to put a period at the end of his last sentence that proudly proclaimed that he finishes everything he starts. He could not believe four years later an admissions officer was willing to correct his punctuation in his essay—hey, admissions people have a sense of humor and we thought this omission was hilarious!

I think that if I attended [college name], I would not add to the arrogance of people who think they will be the greatest person to come to the school since [the founder of the University]. I don't think this attitude is part of the intellectual dimension of [college name], and I hope that isn't the kind of person you are seeking through this essay. What I *do* believe is that the intellectual dimension of [college name] is especially conducive to individual research and innovation; that is the type of work I am most interested in pursuing while in college.

When I am faced with a problem that needs to be solved, I stick with it until I solve it. As an example of this tenacity, I learned to solve Rubik's Cube on my own. While others are looking for the answer sheet, I prefer to attack the problem head-on, knowing there must be a solution if only I try hard enough.

In much the same way, I prefer the challenge of lifting a group or organization which is undeservedly struggling to respectability rather than joining an already successful program. As a freshman, I joined the school band as the only trombone—a situation which remained for the next four years—replacing four who graduated. We also had lost a very popular and capable director in exchange for one whom, to be nice, was not the best. By the next year, we had another new director, and less than 20 remaining members. I stayed in the band, although scheduling conflicts made it difficult, because I thought the band needed me.

Similarly, last year I joined the then-unpopular school newspaper rather than the "prestigious", "elite"—and cliquish—yearbook. I became news editor immediately: there were only six full-time staff members, two of whom really didn't care. I usually did my pages myself, and I strove to make sure they were the best that I could make them. I can accept criticism if I deserve it, but I prefer not to deserve it. Towards the end of last year and the beginning of this year, the paper has really turned around. I have heard no derogatory comments this year, in fact, I have heard some compliments. We also managed to recruit some of the best juniors away from the yearbook: our staff is now 11.

If I attended [college name], I would try to be a credit to its tradition of excellence. I have trouble supporting ideas I don't agree with, but I do everything in my power to promote those I do. If I decide I will accomplish something, I will, even if no one else cares, because I want to prove, if only to myself, that I am capable of finishing anything I start

© JIST Works

Rising to the Challenge of a Creative Essay Question

This essay was written in response to the instruction "write a letter to someone as if you were a job applicant for a job you would like to have." This applicant is now a rather well-known national television personality—mainly sports, but also entertainment.

Cecil B. DeMille, MGM Studios, Hollywood, California

Dear C.B.,

It has come to my attention that you are currently planning a production of "Superman." An excellent choice, old fellow! I should like to wish you the best of luck and much success.

As you know, we go back a long time, dear chap, and I have never been hesitant to offer you hints or suggestions which I feel may be helpful to you in the success of your various productions. I realize that casting begins next week and feel compelled to tell you about a new actress that I have discovered, named Glenda Green. Not a very good name for a Broadway star, I must admit, however, that is but a minor detail, for this girl has potential, C.B.! But be especially watchful of her! Although she lettered on the varsity Track Team as a high-jumper, she is quite incapable of leaping tall buildings in a single bound! Not really the athletic type, you know. However, I feel that she would be wonderful in the role of Lois Lane. Let me tell you about her.

Heavy drama does not suit her taste, so this light, funny musical would be just perfect! Although her name may not be famous yet, she has had a substantial amount of experience in the theater. And I tell you, this kid is moving up the ladder quickly! She has gone from a chorus member in the musicals "Oliver", "A Christmas Musicale", and "Babes in Arms" to leading roles in the productions "Stage Door", "Fiddler on the Roof", and "Plain and Fancy". Miss Green has also attended various workshops and has even been assistant director for the play "Up the Down Staircase." So you see, C.B. she has devoted a considerable amount of her time to the theater and therefore would be equally dedicated to a role in your production.

Although I shall venture to say this girl is not an opera singer, she can belt out showstoppers. Her range *is* somewhat limited, however she compensates for this by singing loudly and energetically. Because of her seven year involvement with various singing groups and her participation in numerous concerts, she has learned sight reading and various singing techniques. She has even become a soloist for her chorale in the past couple of years! Another of her attributes which may be of some interest to you, old pal, is that she is quite artistic. She has taken

(continued)

(continued)

various art courses and things of that sort and is currently engaged in AP Studio Art, whatever that may be! You may find her creativity useful in make up, costuming, or program design. She has had some experience in these areas.

I have just presented you with a basic summary of Miss Green's talents and experiences, C.B.; however I realize that her personality will also be an important factor in your decision. Miss Green, you may as well come to find out, is definitely not the submissive type and is quite unafraid to voice her opinions. The independent sort! However she *can* be made to cooperate and is not unreasonable in any sense. She has also finally learned to keep her priorities in order and to handle the responsibilities of a role, by not neglecting such matters as homework. However, to be quite frank with you, old chap, I think her greatest attribute is her enthusiasm. She has boundless energy and is willing to work hard and to learn as much as possible. She was her school's mascot (head cheerleader) and brought out tremendous school spirit in everyone by her constant energy, great smile and super enthusiasm. She simply loves people and working with them.

I personally feel that it would be a great honor and joy for her to be a member of your cast. She is, indeed, a highly qualified candidate for the part of Lois Lane. Keep an eye out for this one, C.B.!

I remain, respectfully yours,
G. L. Green and Associates, Talent Scout Agent

A Successful Essay and a Successful Student

This student was elected as the student body president of her college in her senior year. She now works in London for a top-level investment banking firm doing creative business research for clients. Instructions for this essay were as follow: "If you were to write a book, on what theme or subject would it be based, and why?"

As long as I can remember my English teachers have told me that the rule to good writing is to "write what you know." Taking their advice into consideration, I would write a piece of literature about an extraordinary family that I became acquainted with when I lived in a small town in central Ohio. This unique family, the Griepenstrohs, (and yes, that was their real name), were so involved in the community that hardly a town function occurred without the Griepenstrohs either planning it or volunteering their spacious Victorian house for the location. The Griepenstrohs were not extraordinary in the sense that they had made important contributions to mankind, or discovered a new gene mutation, or even made a lot of money, but their passion for helping others is what inspired me, and caused me to want to share the example that they set.

© JIST Works

I became best friends with Sally Griepenstroh in fifth grade. We went to the same parochial school and although she was a pale, awkward, and lanky girl, she was the nicest and most thoughtful in our class. The first exposure I had to her parents occurred when I went over to her house to finish a school project on the civil war. As soon as I walked in the door, and made my way through their cluttered home office, being careful not to step on the numerous piles of paper strewn across the floor, her mother, Sue, awaited us. She was so enthused about Sara and I learning every detail about the siege at Vicksburg, one could have guessed she wrote her dissertation solely on this battle. This was only the beginning of Mrs. Griepenstroh's involvement in my education. For the next project, which required Sue and I to construct some sort of mechanical device, she graciously suggested that we use some of the plastic tubes that Mr. Griepenstroh sold. That was the reason for the home office, Mr. Griepenstroh was a plastic tube salesman, and Mrs. Griepenstroh was his assistant. I have no idea what kind of sales volume he did, who knows what the plastic tube market was like seven years ago.

Outside the home though, the Griepenstrohs were just as energetic. On any given day one could find Mr. Griepenstroh mowing the unkempt grass divider between the state highway and the exit to our town, or Mrs. Griepenstroh traveling door to door with her "Neighborhood Restoration Organization: save our precious houses" tee-shirt, distributing pamphlets. During the summer they always organized a sandcastle building contest at the local park. They were the parents that would always volunteer to be chaperones on school field trips, show up to every PTA meeting, and bake those seven dozen brownies for the bake sale. Their selflessness was recognized by all, and respect appropriately came along with that acknowledgement.

The Griepenstrohs were not normal in any sense, one could call them a little "kooky", or off-balanced. Although revered by the community, they also had the reputation of being "weird." Their sense of humor tended to favor witty British comedy. Nevertheless, I would compose an entire book to this Midwestern small town family because I think everyone could learn something from the "amazing Griepenstrohs." They were extremely creative, supportive, and accepting individuals. Their tireless dedication to every aspect of our community taught me that giving can fill one's life. I intend, in my own way, to exhibit such a passion for life.

A Battery of Short-Essay Questions

This student scored 1600 on her SAT and switched majors after one semester from creative writing to theoretical mathematics. She was selected as a Marshall Scholar and is doing graduate work at a major university in England. She plans to get her Ph.D. in theoretical math and become a college professor.

She also lived in a quad freshman year with assigned roommates, two of whom were horrible roommates. In her sophomore and junior years, she got to pick her roommates and was very happy with them.

Following are her responses to multiple short-answer questions of the type that appear on some college application supplements. Frequently, these short-answer responses augment what the candidate provides in the major essay.

Question: Discuss the most important things you want to get out of your college experience.

Most importantly, I don't want my college experience to be easy. I want my college years to make me a better writer, a better learner, and a better teacher. Since none of these improvements come easily, I know that achieving them in college will require effort and determination. These qualities I already have. I hope that my college experience will better equip me to accomplish my main goals in life, which are to become a writer and an English teacher. I have already experienced the joy of passing on valuable knowledge to others through tutoring and teaching piano lessons. I smile with my young students as they first experience the excitement of creating music. College will allow me to share in this same joy every day of my adult life, as I guide my students through the challenges of writing and self-expression. Of course, if I want to be a better teacher, I must first dedicate myself to becoming a better learner. At college, I plan to put enormous effort into improving my own learning, writing, and teaching, fueled by the knowledge that improving myself and my own abilities will someday benefit my students.

Question: Describe something you wish you better understood and why.

I wish I could better understand how single sex cheerleading survived the feminist movement. Sitting on the bleachers in a crowded gymnasium for another useless pep rally, I stare at the offensively short skirts of my long-legged, cheering contemporaries down on the floor. I wonder what Susan B. Anthony and Elizabeth Cady Stanton would think. My ancestors won so many hard-fought battles so teenage girls could wear mini-skirts and entertain fans while their boyfriends play football? Somehow, it just doesn't seem right. With all the sports now available to young girls, why do so many of my peers still choose pom-poms over soccer cleats and batting helmets? Why am I still forced into this gym to watch the girl who discussed literature with me earlier in the day, now shouting a chant with obvious grammatical errors and childish simplicity? Were the general sentiments of society changed without my knowledge in between bells? Many of my classmates do not understand my objections. They are perfectly happy to speak fondly and intelligently of heroines like Joan of Arc one period, and prostrate themselves to the wishes of the mighty, testosterone gods of football the next. They do not see a conflict. I, however, do not see an excuse.

Question: Describe your ideal roommate.

When cooking up an ideal roommate, it is most important not to let the batter get too thin. Any shape, color, and size baking pan will do, for it is the inner ingredients of the dish that must be just right. Firstly, you must put 206 bones and 21 pairs of chromosomes into the pan, if you want your roommate to be human, that is. Hair is optional. Bald roommates cook up just as nicely. Character and honesty are mixed in next. Failure to put in the proper number of spoonfuls of honesty will result in roommates that lie about borrowing your stuff. Memory is also added at this time. One spoonful only. No more, no less. No one wants roommates who forget to deliver messages or remember all your dirty secrets. If you are a musician, especially a bad one, you must also add a pinch of hearing loss so your practicing will not annoy your roommate. A dash of insomnia is also recommended, so your roommate will never insist on turning out the lights before you've finished your homework. Be extremely careful when adding this ingredient, however, because too much will mean you'll have to learn to sleep with the lights on yourself. Lastly, one must not forget to add a cup of tolerance, two tablespoons of friendliness, and a generous helping of compassion, so that your roommate will accept, befriend, and support you in your moments of need. Bake in the oven of college for four years, adding additional years for graduate schooling, adjusting for years lived off campus.

Question: Discuss an experience that taught you something valuable about life.

I remember the exact shoes I was wearing on my way back from the showers on that particular day of summer camp. I remember them because for that brief moment they ceased to be ordinary shoes and transformed into murder weapons. It was Megan who saw it first. I never actually saw it at all, that is, until after I had killed it. Megan was walking right beside me and looking at the adorable baby frog in our path when my foot came crashing down on the poor innocent thing. I felt a slight squish and stopped suddenly as Megan was struck speechless until finally exclaiming in an accusatory tone, "You killed it!"

"Killed what?" I asked, still oblivious. I slowly lifted up my foot to get a look at the bottom of my shoe. The small frog was clearly dead. The bulk of his corpse was staring up at us from the pavement, while the rest of him was securely fastened to the bottom of my shoe. She knew of course that I hadn't seen it. The more important thing, however, was why I hadn't seen it. Megan had seen it. Megan is one of the most observant people I have ever met. I'd always thought of myself as an observant and caring person, but I later realized that I would have seen the frog, too, had I been paying attention. In order to earn our true place in this world we must observe and care for it in a way that goes beyond self-interest. Perhaps if the average person walked just a little more appreciatively and alertly

(continued)

(continued)

> through life, a few frogs would be saved. I doubt that I have learned my full lesson when it comes to noticing and protecting the environment, but to my credit, I saw a frog in my backyard two months ago and I didn't step on it. I am sorry for that frog that died beneath my shoe. I hope he can forgive me and find comfort in the fact that at least his death meant enough to me to open my eyes. The best I can do for him now is promise never to close them again.

Other Trends and Insights from the Admission Experts

With the student applicant pool for the graduating class of 2012 expected to be the largest ever, competition will continue to be fierce into institutions at nearly every level—from the top-tier and most selective colleges nationwide to the large state universities and virtually every college in between.

Some of our admission professionals share their takes on the changing landscape within college admissions and provide further advice on how to navigate the competitive applicant fields of candidates.

Increasingly More Qualified Applicants

Jean Jordan, Interim Dean of Admission, Emory University, said "There have been numerous changes among the applicant pools over the past few years: Not just in size, but in terms of selectivity and the caliber of students we are seeing. In the most recent year, more than 15,000 applications were submitted to Emory, of which fewer than 4,500 students will be accepted (for a first-year class size of about 1,255)."

- **Colleges working to make students happy with their choice:** Jeanne Jenkins (Rensselaer) stated that "colleges do a wonderful job for the students they serve. The biggest challenge with high school kids is getting them to a point that regardless of where they *thought* was their first choice, they drive proudly to their chosen school with the (institution's) decal on their cars' back windows. The process of getting there shouldn't be as angst-ridden as we've all made it."

- **Deferring entrance:** Another trend noted by Jean Jordan (Emory) is that more students than ever before are deferring entrance to college—once garnering their acceptances, they opt to defer entrance for a year—to pursue AmeriCorps opportunities, recover from having worn themselves out with high academic achievements their junior and senior years in high school, and for a variety of other reasons.

- **Deferring decisions:** Jean Jordan also pointed out that when it comes to the university deferring a decision on a student (in other words, wait-listing), at least at Emory, the prospects are not especially encouraging. For the 2006–2007 academic year, no one was subsequently admitted from the wait list; for the year before, just 25 students were admitted from wait-list status. To improve the odds of a student moving from wait-listed status to accepted, Ms. Jordan suggested the following communications strategy: "There is relevance to communicating what they've done in the recent months (of senior year) to enhance their candidacy. They should stay in contact with someone on the admissions staff who can be a conduit for this type of information. It's important to show what they've accomplished in the interim and what they have achieved of value."

Adding Veracity to the Essay: Writing Samples

Don Bishop, Associate Vice President for Enrollment Management, Creighton University, explains the new importance of writing scores on standardized tests: "The SAT/ACT writing sample and score is now favored by many colleges because it allows the college to see what a student can write in a limited amount of time with a guarantee that the effort is authentic and solely developed by the student. The proliferation of manufactured essays through the assistance of the Internet and consultants was the root cause for the change and requirement from many colleges. How well a student writes and how well they can develop their thoughts and demonstrate deep thinking is important to the colleges. A quality piece of writing and thinking is still a very important part of the selection process. Colleges just want to make sure the essays are written by the student."

- **Students attempting to use the essay to excuse poor classroom performance:** At the University of Rhode Island, Eric Simonelli stated that he has seen an increase in students attempting to write stellar essays as a means by which "to excuse poor performance in the classroom. For example, if a student is an average 'C' student and he or she writes an especially well-developed essay, he or she thinks that essay can automatically enhance the chances of being accepted. We look primarily at the high school transcript and the courses the student has taken—and how well he or she has performed in those courses. It is important to take seriously the writing of an essay; but it is also just as important to understand that students are evaluated holistically on a wide range of criteria."

- **More emphasis on student interest:** Gil Villanueva (Brandeis) reported on a recent trend observed by the National Association for College Admission Counseling: "More and more admissions offices are accounting for the level of demonstrated interest (called the DI factor)." As a result, there are more applicants willing to disclose their level of interest about a particular college in their essays.

- **Increasing competition:** Douglas Christiansen (Vanderbilt) reflected on seeing a "100 percent change over the years," driven by the continually increased competition. "Students from affluent private or public high schools begin thinking about the college admissions process much earlier and are making decisions on the basis of what will help them get into the 'right' college. Students in 10th grade are making choices about extracurricular activities on the basis of what will boost their resume or admissions application. The pressure on young people today has grown exponentially."

- **Private counselors:** Rice University's vice president for enrollment, Chris Muñoz, commented on an interesting trend in the admissions world. "The biggest change now is that because there is so much competition for a relatively small number of slots at the most select universities, there has been an upsurge of a cottage industry. Private counselors and companies are now available to assist individuals who are highly motivated to gain acceptance into some of the nation's top institutions. Some of the approaches used are very slick and don't always work in a student's best interest, however. I urge all students to consider this: If the approach being recommended or used is really outside the box, be very careful. Does it truly represent you well— and as you wish to be represented?"

© JIST Works

What Makes for an Effective Essay?

Vince Cuseo, Dean of Admission, Occidental College, on the characteristics of an effective essay: "Although there are essays that receive universal praise, students may be surprised by the range of opinion about essays within a given admission office. Effective writing is valuable—even critical—in any profession. It behooves colleges to seek ways to evaluate and improve student writing.

That said, are our expectations of an applicant's writing competency realistic? Isn't college the setting in which writing should be honed? I'm less moved by impeccably constructed but inert essays than raw, deeply revelatory ones. I prefer substance—as defined by gaining a peek into an applicant's life and personality—over style, i.e., an essay that has near-perfect syntax and diction but leaves me with no insight. Of course, I prefer both! In the end, effective essays are a melding of clear, persuasive writing and honest unveiling."

Key Points: Chapter 3

- The best assistance you can get with your college essay is to ask trusted advisors (parents, guidance counselors, English teachers) to review what you have already written.

- Although some institutions may offer feedback about your essay, at the time they do so (following receipt of your application), it is too late to make any substantive changes in how you present yourself as a prospective student. Therefore, take the time upfront to plan, write, and proofread your resume carefully *before* submitting it.

- In addition to the excellent and inspiring collection of diverse student-written essays in chapter 7, the small group of admission dean–selected essays in this chapter gives some good examples of what to do—and what not to do—when considering your own essay-writing approach.

- Admission pros consistently advise students to be themselves—but polished and persuasive—in writing their essays. As the competition stiffens for colleges at all levels, you must present your true self in the best possible light for your application to get that second look.

Chapter 4

Quick Steps for Crafting an Essay in an Hour

Don't think you can actually write your essay in an hour? In this chapter, you'll see how it's really possible. Turn to page 70 for the steps and timetable for producing an essay in just 60 minutes. It helps to have had an opportunity to read not only the contents of this chapter but the entire book before attempting this exercise. But if you're really under the gun, flip ahead and jump right in. If you have a little more time, it will make more sense to read the details of some of the key steps—whether you want to produce an essay in an hour or over the summer following your junior year of high school.

Up to this point in the book, you have been reading excellent recommendations for refining, polishing, and focusing your essay—all from the admission experts. You'll also find in chapter 5 extensive advice from students who, just a year or so ago, were sitting where you are now. They share their best strategies for writing essays and how they used them to garner college acceptance. Here's the blueprint to follow in writing your application essay.

Essay Basics

Drawing on a wealth of information as provided through actual student experiences and the informed opinions of admissions deans from respected schools around the country, the following is a quick checklist for writing your college application essay using an approach created by Paul Marthers, the Dean of Admission at Reed College, as the foundation.

1. **Plan on writing two essays:** a) the Common Application or a more general question; and b) an essay that speaks to specifically why you are interested in a particular university.

2. **Make sure the essay is tailored to the college, not written generically as a one-version-fits-all.** Proofread to make sure the correct college name appears in the essay (especially likely to be a problem if you cut-and-paste the same essay for many schools).

3. **Write what only you can write.** The essay is you, captured on paper in one to four pages (and usually two pages or less). Consider, when reading your first draft, whether you think what you have written could be about someone else. Or—ideally—is it unmistakably you?

4. **Follow the guidelines.** Be sure to follow the exact directions provided by the institution: If it says 500 words, try not to exceed that count (generally, admissions deans stated that a very well-written and carefully edited essay that was 520 words wouldn't hurt the applicant). If the directions indicate one page for a response (application question or essay), be sure to stay within the one page. The key thing is to follow guidelines and instructions explicitly.

5. **Think first.** Think about what it is you wish to convey about yourself to the admission committee.

6. **Get feedback on your message.** After you have written a draft, hand the essay to someone else and ask the person to give you a two- to four-sentence verbal summary. Is the summary congruent with the message you want to transmit with your essay? If not, rework the essay. If so, refine it to a final draft.

7. **Know that there is no magic formula.** There is no magic formula for a winning essay. Admission committees can't exactly define the qualities of an exceptional essay, but like former U.S. Supreme Court Justice Potter Stewart said about obscenity, "I know it when I see it."

8. **Know that there is no perfect topic.** There are no topics that get attention more than other topics. Applicants who try to find a winning topic often choose one that has been done many, many times before. Instead, be yourself.

9. **Be authentic.** Admission committees know that you are 16 to 18 years old and have not won a Nobel Prize, competed in the Olympics, or discovered a cure for cancer. You are going to their college to expand your knowledge and vault toward future impressive accomplishments. The committee wants an authentic glimpse into your individual world.

Questions to Get You Started (or at Least Thinking Creatively)

You've probably done writing prompts (fill-in-the-blank questions to get you started writing) in your English classes throughout much of high school. See whether any of the following prompts proves inspirational in getting you "off the dime" and writing. Feel free to substitute different ages or levels where needed to tell your story. The idea isn't to copy these as the actual beginning of your essay—but to use the prompt to think, "Oh, yeah, *that* would be a good topic for me to discuss!" Then write fully in your own words, letting your ideas flow.

- From the time that I was [10 years old, 12 years old, in middle school…], I always knew that I was destined to study _____.

- Ever since I was [10, 12, in middle school…], I have wanted to _____.

- I have known that for at least the past [5, 8, 10…] years, I would find a way to [study, pursue, become] _____.

- Some people love [music, art, playing sports, videogames, studying history]; however, I love _____.

- Did you ever wonder how [_____] came to be?

- I've always been curious and that's why science has been my favorite subject since I was in seventh grade.

- I have always imagined [_____].

- I have always dreamed about [_____].

- I have always planned to [study, pursue, use my skills with] [math/foreign language].

- Some people find that [_____]; I [_____].

- I have always believed that if you want something badly enough, you [_____].

- I have always believed in the expression "where there is a will, there's a way."

- I didn't start out believing that I could make a difference. But in my experience as a [volunteer, runner, _____], I learned what one person does really can have an impact on the lives of others.

- People who know me say that I am one of the [funniest, most outgoing, _____] people they know. What people don't know about me is that I am actually very shy. I've learned to compensate….

- Something my teachers have always said about me is that I really know how to apply myself—especially when faced with something new and particularly demanding. I think that is why I have:

- Been drawn to the study of [_____]...

   Or:

- Always challenged myself by taking the more difficult classes. Even if it meant foregoing an *A* in a top-level regular class, I wanted the challenge of an AP class where I might be able to earn only a *B*, but would have the opportunity to really stretch myself and learn more.

- Some people have said that it's a real accomplishment to have played a varsity sport through four years of high school while earning good grades. For me, it has been the discipline and time-management skills I've learned as a result of balancing practice, games, studying, and academic work that has been the real achievement. *[Could this apply to something you do?]*

The Creative Writing Process

Let your creativity flow. Completely resist the urge to edit at this point. If ideas are starting to come to you rapidly, try to get them all down on paper. You can worry about the ones to discard and the ones on which to build in just a bit. For now, it's key to unleash the creativity you have about whatever topic(s) is buzzing in your head.

The rest of this section details the most important steps in the creative writing process: framing the essay, refining its appearance, and then editing and revising what you've written.

Framing the Essay

You already know from expository writing, report writing, and the like that you need a good outline to write well. Time is limited, so you're not going to spend a lot of time on this. Nonetheless, try to capture some of the key points you'd like to weave into this essay.

You probably want to strive for an essay in the 250- to 300-word range (less if there is a specific restriction for the school for which you are writing this—and more if you wish and if the school accepts 500 words or more).

> **Tip:** *If you have time, review the do's and don'ts presented by admission experts in chapter 2 and other advice about applications in chapter 3. Chapters 6 and 7 also feature excellent advice from students now in college—based on when they were high school seniors and writing their own application essays.*

© JIST Works

Introduction

You need to start somewhere. Sometimes the best place to begin writing your essay is not at the literal beginning. You can always go back when editing to move things around or add a solid opening. But, for now, try to put down on paper a few phrases that you think could serve to start off your essay.

Body

This is the key section of your essay where you'll really tell the story and present the most important details. You can decide whether this section lends itself to subsections. For instance, with expository writing, you can start with the following in your rough draft:

> "First, …"

Then in the next paragraph, you might begin with

> "Next, …"

And in the closing paragraph of the body, you could say

> "Finally, …"

This isn't necessarily the most creative way you could go; it's just for starters. Don't feel constrained to use this style; it is one of many approaches.

Conclusion

This is where you wrap things up, tie ideas together, and—ideally—come up with a compelling closing that communicates the message you want to share.

Most editors say that your introduction and your conclusion are the most important parts of your essay.

- The introduction is essential to capture the reader's interest and provide enough information in a captivating way that entices the reader to continue reading into the body.

- The body, of course, is important because it advances the story. The pace should move the reader to the next points.

- The conclusion is nearly as important as the introduction because this is where you leave the reader with a "call to action" or memorable image. It's where you "close the deal."

Refining the Essay's Appearance

First and foremost, always follow the directions. (This is probably the second or third time that you've read that in this book, and there's a good reason for that.) If the college asks for a single 8.5" × 11" sheet of paper with double-spaced content, do that. You might be given a word limit. Try to the best of your ability to stay within the limit allowed. If the directions say to single-space the content, do that. If there are details regarding font ("no smaller than 12 points" or "Times New Roman only"), adhere to those guidelines.

Whether you have an hour, a weekend, or the entire summer, ensure that you proofread very carefully. Don't simply rely on spell-check—it doesn't always catch the incorrect use of a homonym (you typed *their* but meant *there*) or dropped word endings.

Consider the following comments from Don Bishop, Associate Vice President for Enrollment Management, Creighton University: "Too many students ignore the opportunity to use the essay as a personal opportunity and instead of writing an essay, they write a report which lists their high school activities and their college goals. *An essay tells the reader not only about the activity or thoughts that are most important to you but also why they are important to you.* When I read an essay, I want to know why a student did what they chose to write about and what they learned from doing this activity. I often expect that the essay will tell me whether the student has the ability to think deeply or just on the surface—not only about themselves but others and the world. A well-written essay tells the admissions officer not only what you think about yourself, but also what you think about others and how you relate to people and the world."

Editing and Revising

Other than proofreading, editing and revising are among the most important steps in producing a quality essay. Anecdotal evidence from high school English teachers and college English professors suggests that editing is one of the most frequently lacking skills among students today. Sentiments range from "students think once they've written the paper and spell-checked it, they're done" to "Editing? Revising? The terms appear to be an unknown foreign language to many students today."

As a lifelong writer—and writer by profession for several decades—I can attest to the fact that good editing is almost more important than good writing. Why? A quality editing job can fix even marginal writing, and it's rare for any individual to produce absolutely perfect work the first time through. Tightening copy, deleting clichés, improving syntax, eliminating choppiness, correcting punctuation, checking spelling, removing redundancies—you will accomplish all of these steps in editing; however, you shouldn't really consider them at all in the writing of the first draft.

When it comes to editing the essay, this means more than just proofreading (which, you know already *ad infinitum,* is terribly essential). It means putting a document aside for a long enough period of time to cool—and then coming back to it with fresh eyes and renewed perspective. It is picking up that cooled document and really reading it for new meaning. This allows your eye to see the holes, notice the mistakes (that your eyes would naturally smooth over and fill in if you proofed it immediately after you wrote a piece). Even professional proofreaders have difficulty proofing their own work—unless they give it a little time to settle.

As you read through your work out loud (this step is very important: It allows you to hear how the piece flows and really sounds), ask yourself the following questions:

- If I knew nothing about the subject matter, would the essay make sense to me?

- What is the message I'm really conveying?

- How does the tone sound?

- Are there any awkward sentences or poorly constructed phrases?

- Am I left wanting to know something more? (Worse, am I just left hanging?)

- Is it interesting? Or is the piece boring? (Be honest.)

- Does the essay look like I'm trying too hard to be funny, entertaining, or witty?

- Does it sound natural?

- Is it too wordy or filled with too many adjectives and/or SAT test–worthy words?

- Do I like the person described in the essay?

Of course, it is difficult to be objective in responding to these questions. But here an outside editor can be of help: you can invite a parent, an older brother or sister, a favorite teacher, or even a guidance counselor to take a look and consider the essay from a variety of perspectives. Ask these advisors to consider your essay from the standpoint of the preceding questions.

Only after completing the serious work of editing, revising, and proofreading can you really say that your essay is complete and ready to submit. This is an incredibly satisfying feeling—and you should feel very proud of your labors when you get to that point!

One-Hour College Application Essay Writing Exercise

It's crunch time. It happens to everyone (occasionally). For the most part, we'll assume that you have methodically planned your college search process, including development of at least draft versions of your college application essays. But suppose the computer crashed…the dog ate all your printouts…you woke up one morning with total amnesia…and you realize that today is the final deadline to pull together an application for one of your chosen schools. It's Saturday morning. For purposes of this chapter's premise and exercise, we'll presume you are mailing a hard copy of the application and that your post office closes at noon. You need 15 minutes to drive to the post office, and it is now 10:45.

So, as the title on this book's cover suggests, you are seriously in need of a *One-Hour College Application Essay.* There's no time to waste—no time at all, really, for something this important. But I promise to give you a crash course in getting together a college application essay in one hour. It is not my recommendation, however, that you should actually use this essay—not without serious review, editing, setting aside, and buffing.

However, if you are someone who is motivated to work under the gun and find this approach inspiring and helpful in getting you jump-started, you might just want to try this exercise, even if you don't really need to have the essay complete in one hour. It will create an excellent foundation for an essay you might actually choose to use in the admissions process.

© JIST Works

Use the blanks in the worksheets to jot down ideas—preferably the first things that come to mind. No idea is too ridiculous. Don't play editor (yet).

First of all, this is your schedule—the timetable you'll need to pay close attention to in order to do this in 60 minutes. You might find a desktop clock or watch with an alarm helpful to time your work through each section of the exercise.

Steps to a One-Hour Essay	
Steps	*Time Allowed*
1. Select a topic.	5 minutes
2. Brainstorm initial responses.	5 minutes
3. Complete your outline.	10 minutes
4. Focus on the introduction.	10 minutes
5. Write the body next.	10 minutes
6. Wrap up with a conclusion.	10 minutes
7. Read for flow and consistency and write a title.	5 minutes
8. Spell-check by computer and visually proofread.	5 minutes
	Total: 60 minutes

STEP 1: Select a Topic (5 Minutes)

Let's get started. For the one-hour essay, there are three quick-start processes outlined in this section. Briefly read each of the three and then decide which one you think you can tackle.

Answer the following questions as completely as possible. Again, jot down the first thoughts that pop into your mind. This exercise can sometimes be a little difficult (some folks simply aren't comfortable tooting their own horn). But if you think about how someone else would describe you to an individual who doesn't know you, it can get the wheels turning about the things people say about you.

ONE-HOUR ESSAY OPTION #1

What are the three key characteristics about you that you know to be true? Give an example or two of each trait.

1. _____

_____

_____

_____

2. _____

_____

_____

_____

3. _____

_____

_____

_____

ONE-HOUR ESSAY OPTION #2

From the following four questions (all about you), select one for which the most ideas spring to mind and zero in on that.

1. How would your favorite teacher describe you?

_____

_____

_____

© JIST Works

_____

_____

_____

_____

2. How would your coach/art teacher/music instructor/mentor describe you?

_____

_____

_____

_____

_____

_____

3. If you have a part-time job (or had one last summer), how would your boss describe you?

_____

_____

_____

_____

_____

4. If you volunteer/write for the school newspaper/participate in a club or other activity regularly, how would your supervisor/advisor describe you?

_____

_____

(continued)

(continued)

_____

_____

_____

_____

_____

ONE-HOUR ESSAY OPTION #3

Let's say someone is writing a one-paragraph biography about you—describing you to a completely new audience. Picture yourself about to go for a two-month stay at a place you've always wanted to visit (a ski resort in Breckenridge…a Greek villa in the Mediterranean…a mountaintop lake in Switzerland…a fashion studio in Milan). Presume everyone reading this biography understands English perfectly—and that no one has ever met you or heard about you.

What kinds of things would you want this biography to say about who you are today? Try to be as authentic as possible, describing yourself as you really think you are—including those traits and characteristics for which you believe you are known by those who truly know you.

_____

_____

_____

_____

_____

_____

_____

© JIST Works

```
_____
_____
_____
```

STEP 2: Brainstorm Initial Responses (5 Minutes)

Thinking of your chosen topic (one of the three above—or one of your own choosing) and either using the form provided with the question or a pad of your own paper or a blank document on your computer, spend no more than five minutes writing down everything that relates to this topic that springs to mind. Again, resist the urge to play editor. Don't say to yourself, "Oh, that's stupid or ridiculous." The key to good brainstorming is to generate as many ideas as possible (good or otherwise!).

STEP 3: Complete Your Outline (10 Minutes)

Using the following form and the notes you took in brainstorming, start to determine "what goes where." Take your raw ideas and begin to think where they might logically work. Would this thought make a possible opening? Is this idea a good conclusion? Are these some of the steps or series of ideas/events you might write about in the body? Don't worry about spelling, grammar, or sentence structure now. In fact, I recommend *not* writing sentences at this stage. You just want to work to create as thorough an outline as possible—you have 10 minutes!

Introduction

```
_____
_____
_____
_____
```

(continued)

(continued)

_____

_____

_____

Body

_____

_____

_____

_____

_____

_____

_____

Conclusion

_____

_____

_____

_____

_____

_____

_____

STEP 4: Focus on the Introduction (10 Minutes)

Now, with the outline complete, really zero in on the notes you've developed for your introduction. Does something jump out as a possible way to begin the essay? Can you think of some of the strategies and techniques you've read about elsewhere in this book and use those ideas to help you shape your own good ideas? Think about the significant writing you've done throughout your years in school. When faced with a blank page (but, in this case, you've also got two tools available: your completed outline and

© JIST Works

your list of brainstorming thoughts), what do you do first? Maybe consider asking a question—either on paper or of yourself. Jump into the middle of the story you are going to tell—or even go to the ending. You can use the body and conclusion to fill in the back story and make your point.

Spend no more than 10 minutes on the introduction. If you really can't seem to jump into the beginning, move quickly over to the body of the essay. Tell the story first and then go back and think how you can begin the story with an introduction that draws the reader in.

STEP 5: Write the Body (10 Minutes)

This is the core of the story. It's what you've set up in your introduction. And it's what will bring you to the close. What happened? What are you trying to convey? Why is it important? How did you feel? Ask yourself the many questions a total stranger would who wants to know more about you and this event/situation/story you are telling.

Again, you have just 10 minutes for this part of the exercise. There's still no need to worry about editing yet. Try to get the narrative flow to your story on paper.

STEP 6: Wrap Up with a Conclusion (10 Minutes)

Now move to the conclusion. What did you learn? What was the result? Again, how did you feel? What did you think? What did you learn? What would you do differently? Depending on the story you have told, any of these might apply—or none. Come up with your own questions. If someone else had told the same story, what would you want to know of them? Be objective—try to distance yourself from your story so that you can ask yourself questions that will get at your thought process and perspective.

You've got 10 minutes to develop a conclusion. Write as quickly as possible. Try to think of a conclusion that will create a sense of closure—or, if you are feeling more creative, one that begs the next question. Maybe it's a story of how you ended up deciding on your major. Perhaps it will obviously lend itself to a nice wrap-up. On the other hand, maybe you are just starting an exploration or adventure—and have no idea where it will lead. You can end without a definitive, neatly tied package. But you need to be careful that the essay doesn't just drop off into nothingness. It should be clear to the reader that you consciously meant to stop exactly where you did. That's where the occasional question at the end can work effectively.

Play with several techniques—in the 10 minutes you have. When the alarm goes off or your clock shows that 10 minutes have passed, you've got to move on.

STEP 7: Read for Flow and Consistency and Write the Title (5 Minutes)

Going back to the top, read through now for content and flow. Obviously, if you see apparent errors, you can correct them as you go (thus combining partially with step #8). See if the segues are nice and smooth and move the reader along comfortably. Is anything missing? Is the point clear? Will the reader know what you are trying to say? From all that you developed in your outline, consider whether you have clearly articulated the theme of this essay, the whole point. This theme or main idea that you've attempted to convey should help you create a title for the piece.

Not all application essays must have titles. If you are really stuck for a creative title and it is not required, simply leave it off. No title (when not requested) is better than something uninspired, such as "My College Application Essay."

STEP 8: Spell-Check by Computer and Visually Proofread (5 Minutes)

If you weren't proofreading as you read through the first time, now is the time—in your final five minutes—to thoroughly proofread the essay.

Double-check spelling of any words that you're unsure of (using a real dictionary), including those that may have "cleared" spell-check. Look to see that the paragraphing makes sense—not too many short, choppy paragraphs, but no really long blocks of narrative, either. For the most part, following the expository guidelines, you'll probably have one introductory paragraph, two or three paragraphs to the body, and one concluding paragraph.

> **Tip:** Remember that proofreading is absolutely essential.

That's it. Congratulations. You have crafted an application essay in one hour. Now, if you really didn't need to mail that essay at 12 noon today, I strongly suggest putting it aside to cool for at least a day or two. Then go back to it and read it with fresh eyes. Revisit the brainstorming notes you took. Look once again at your outline. Are there other ideas you could bring out in the essay that would strengthen your message? Are you satisfied with the direction it is going? Is it reflecting who you are and what you think you want to say?

This is the time to play serious editor—and feel free to totally scrap the essay if you're not satisfied with its shape, tone, or direction. You can use the same exercise repeatedly (use different questions) to get you started. Or, you can jump into one of the many questions presented in chapter 5 to give you a truly new start on your application essay.

You'll also find numerous additional recommendations from your former peers (college students that were sitting in your chair just a year or two ago) in chapters 5 and 7.

Key Points: Chapter 4

- You need a good roadmap for writing your college essay, especially if you are under the gun of a deadline. If the college application asks you to select from specific questions, make the choice that best allows you to give the most authentic and interesting response. If you can use an open-ended topic, consider a variety of ideas before making your choice.

- Creative-writing prompts can be helpful in getting something onto a blank page. Use the many questions in this chapter to tap your own creativity.

- Consider the key steps in writing: Frame the essay with an introduction, body, and conclusion; determine the appearance; edit and revise; and thoroughly proofread.

- Ready-set-go: Follow key strategies and a time-outlined plan to write a well-developed college application essay in just 60 minutes, from start to finish.

Chapter 5

Actual Essay Questions for Practice—Plus Student Advice

With more time to contemplate, write, and edit, you should feel less anxiety. Keep in mind that the other chapters of this book provide excellent recommendations from the admission experts *and* the college students who adhered to their own advice (or share from the mistakes they learned) in writing their essays. So be sure to read those as well.

The Common Application: First-Year Application for Undergraduate College Admissions

The Common Application is accepted by many colleges and universities—but not all. Schools that indicate that the Common Application is acceptable (they are member schools) make no distinction between it and the school's own application. Some schools do require a supplemental application form and this will be noted both on the school's own Web site (click to the admissions area and then select the "how to apply" category) as well as on the application paperwork.

The 2006–2007 Common Application includes both a short-answer question and a personal-essay requirement. For the short answer, students are asked the following:

> *Please briefly elaborate on one of your activities (extracurricular, personal activities, or work experience). Attach your response on a separate sheet (150 words or fewer).*

Material for this section is based on The Common Application for 2006–2007 (©2006 The Common Application, Inc.).

Students are given a choice of six personal-essay topics on the Common Application. The directions state

This personal statement helps us become acquainted with you in ways different from courses, grades, test scores, and other objective data. It will demonstrate your ability to organize thoughts and express yourself. We are looking for an essay that will help us know you better as a person and as a student. Please write an essay (250–500 words) on a topic of your choice or on one of the options listed below.

The six choices include the following:

- Evaluate a significant experience, achievement, risk you have taken, or ethical dilemma you have faced and its impact on you.

- Discuss some issue of personal, local, national, or international concern and its importance to you.

- Indicate a person who has had a significant influence on you and describe that influence.

- Describe a character in fiction, a historical figure, or a creative work (as in art, music, science, etc.) that has had an influence on you and explain that influence.

- A range of academic interests, personal perspectives, and life experiences adds much to the educational mix. Given your personal background, describe an experience that illustrates what you would bring to the diversity in a college community or an encounter that demonstrated the importance of diversity to you.

- Topic of your choice.

A number of colleges require you to complete one or more supplemental documents in addition to the Common Application. These include everything from providing an athletic supplement document and perhaps game tapes to completing an arts supplement and providing a portfolio or CD. Supplemental applications can be very concise and short (one or two pages in length) or all encompassing (for example, Duke University's supplement is 10 pages long). Within the supplemental applications, at least half of all schools also require additional essays (beyond what is required on the Common Application).

© JIST Works

A sampling of the type of questions is given later in the chapter, including the names of some of the schools asking these questions. Where more than one question is listed for a particular school, the applicant usually must choose to answer just one query. Where essays are required of specific students (usually based on intended major) or are optional to a specific program, that information is noted.

> **Note:** *Many schools use very similar if not identical supplemental questions.*

Deciding on an Essay Topic

Without question this is the number-one problem cited by high school juniors and seniors. Thoughts such as these might be going through your head:

What should I write about?

Nothing I've done is very important or interesting.

I have no idea what to say.

No one could possibly be interested in what I think I'd want to write about.

And so on and so on.

In addition to the exercises in chapter 4, this chapter presents many different approaches—straightforward, creative, experimental, and fun—for getting at an answer to this perplexing question. Let's get started.

Essay Questions from Actual Applications

Many schools offer applicants a choice of four or five questions. Often, the final question allows you to write on a topic of your choosing. In addition to essay questions, a number of schools use a supplemental application that might include one or more short-answer questions.

Most of the questions that follow have been extracted from actual college applications available on the Internet through the respective school's Web site (each school and its URL is identified accordingly). Questions are categorized based on commonality of themes to illustrate the subtle and sometimes overt differences similar topics can have. Where a school is not identified in parentheses following a question, the topic is generic in nature or is one that I use in my private practice with students.

Favorite Book

- The counselors, student interns, and staff in our office keep a running reading list. If you could contribute one book to the list, which would it be and why? (Bennington College, www.bennington.edu)

- Consider the books, essays, poems, or journal articles you have read over the last year or two, either for school or leisure. Please discuss the way in which one of them has changed your understanding of the world, other people, or yourself. Please limit your response to one to three paragraphs. (Duke University, www.duke.edu)

> **Tip:** *You may like several of these actual questions that different colleges and universities around the country use. For an open-ended essay on a topic of your choosing for any university, these questions might be just the key to triggering the creative juices and helping you zero in on a topic on which to base your essay.*

- From your reading, whether Dr. Seuss or Chaucer, what books or authors have particularly impressed you? (Carleton College, www.carleton.edu)

- The late scholar James O. Freedman referred to libraries as "essential harbors on the voyage toward understanding ourselves." What work of fiction or nonfiction would you include in a personal library? Why? (Tufts University, www.tufts.edu)

- Think about the books you have read during your high school years (inside and outside of the classroom); rank the three best in order. Explain the reason for your top selection. (Simmons College, www.simmons.edu)

IT'S YOUR TURN

Write about one of your favorite books and share why the book made an impression on you. Jot down your preliminary ideas here.

_____

_____

_____

© JIST Works

```
_____
_____
_____
```

Subject or Program Specific

- **Engineering:** Please discuss why you want to study engineering and why you would like to study at Duke. Please limit your response to one to three paragraphs. (Duke University, Pratt School of Engineering, www.pratt.duke.edu/about/index.php)

- **Arts and Sciences:** Please discuss why you consider Duke a good match for you. Is there something in particular at Duke that attracts you? Please limit your response to one to three paragraphs. (Duke University, Trinity College of Arts and Sciences, www.aas.duke.edu/trinity/research/)

- **Journalism:** Write a profile of yourself in news or news feature style, as if you had interviewed yourself. (George Washington University, www.gwu.edu)

- **Political Communication:** If you could be any one person who has been active in politics, who would you choose to be and why? (George Washington University, www.gwu.edu)

- **Architecture:** Please respond to each of the following:

  1. What aspirations, experiences, or relationships have motivated you to pursue the study of architecture?

  2. Outside of academics, what do you enjoy most or find most challenging? Responses to each section should be approximately one page. (Rice University, www.rice.edu)

It's Your Turn

What draws you to this particular field of interest? (If you have no idea which particular college within a university is right for you, that's perfectly fine—and typical of about 70 percent of high school

(continued)

(continued)

seniors. You would not select this as an essay question, obviously!) Jot down your preliminary ideas here.

_____

_____

_____

_____

_____

_____

Academic Program Choice

- With the understanding that the choice of academic school you indicated is not binding, explain why you are applying to that particular school of study. (Rice University, www.rice.edu)

- We would like to know, in no more than 500 words, what experiences have led you to select your professional field and objective. (Boston University, www.bu.edu)

- What subjects most interest you and why? (Carleton College, www.carleton.edu)

- Name a professor with whom you would like to study or conduct research and explain why. (University of Pennsylvania, www.upenn.edu)

It's Your Turn

What interests you about studying your selected field? (If you have no idea what your major will be, that's perfectly fine—and typical of about 70 percent of high school seniors. You would not select this as an essay question, obviously!) Jot down your preliminary ideas here.

_____

_____

Most Interesting Work or Educational Experience

- Describe your most interesting work *or* educational experience. (Rice University, www.rice.edu)

- Briefly tell us about an academic class, teacher, research project, or other educational experience in secondary school that has been significant for you. (Kenyon College, www.kenyon.edu)

- Describe an event, experience, or cultural interaction that has prepared you to work and lead in a global community. (Washington State University, www.wsu.edu)

- Is your past academic record an accurate reflection of your ability and potential? Please elaborate on your answer. (College of the Atlantic, www.coa.edu)

- By this point in your academic career, you have taken a variety of courses, each with its own distinguishing characteristics. Which one has had the most influence on your interests and goals for the future and why? (Johns Hopkins University, www.jhu.edu)

- Did you pursue a topic or topics in high school with real personal enthusiasm? What do your teachers tell us about your engagement with a topic? (Wesleyan University, www.wesleyan.edu)

IT'S YOUR TURN

Share a story about your most interesting work experience (or educational experience). Jot down your preliminary ideas here.

(continued)

87

(continued)

_____

_____

_____

_____

Life Experience

- Tell us about an experience in which you left your comfort zone. How did this experience change you? (University of Richmond, www.ur.edu)

- If you have spent a recent summer in a service project, study program, or work or travel opportunity, please describe. (Kenyon College, www.kenyon.edu)

- First experiences can be defining. Cite a first experience that you have had and explain its impact on you. (University of Pennsylvania, www.upenn.edu)

- Describe the environment in which you were raised—your family, home, neighborhood, or community—and how it influenced the person you are today. (Tufts University, www.tufts.edu)

- Did you engage in a community or school activity that shows enthusiasm for acting collectively? Have you developed leadership qualities? (Wesleyan University, www.wesleyan.edu)

- Relate an event or situation in your life where your personal sense of honor influenced you or guided your actions. (University of Mary Washington, www.umw.edu)

- Recall an occasion when you took a risk that you now know was the right thing to do. (University of Pennsylvania, www.upenn.edu)

- Please take a moment to consider the role of learning, in or out of class, in your own life. Then, write an essay (250–500 words) sharing your thoughts with us. Please don't feel that you need to base your

© *JIST Works*

essay on the quotations below. They are simply meant to give you a place from which to start. Remember that this is your chance to take a subject on which every applicant is writing and make it your own.

- "There are two types of education.... One should teach us how to make a living, and the other how to live." —John Adams

- "...for education amongst all kinds of men always has had, and always will have, an element of danger and revolution, of dissatisfaction and discontent. Nevertheless, men strive to know." —W.E.B. DuBois

- "For the sole true end of education is simply this: To teach men how to learn for themselves; and whatever instruction fails to do this is effort spent in vain." —Dorothy Sayers

- "I can't believe it! Reading and writing actually paid off!" —Homer Simpson

(Sarah Lawrence College, www.slc.edu)

- As a Catholic University committed to building a more inclusive community, USD values students with diverse backgrounds and experiences. Briefly explain how your unique background and interests will contribute to our community. (University of San Diego, www.sandiego.edu)

- How do you envision your studies at COA fitting in with your overall educational and career goals? (College of the Atlantic, www.coa.edu)

- Gettysburg College students take pride in "making a difference" both on and off campus through their academic and extracurricular activities. Describe a situation in which you have made a difference in your school or community and what you learned from that experience. (Gettysburg College, www.gettysburg.edu)

- Describe a moment in which you took a risk and achieved an unexpected goal. How did you persuade others to follow your lead? What lessons do you draw from this experience? You may reflect on examples from your academic, extracurricular, or athletic experiences. (Tufts University, www.tufts.edu)

It's Your Turn

What is one of your more interesting or course-changing life experiences? Jot down your preliminary ideas here.

_____

_____

_____

_____

_____

_____

Creative Expression

- *The following question is asked as part of the application. There is a box approximately 3 inches wide by 2¾ inches high. The directions indicate the following:* Fill the box to the right with something that appeals to you. (Rice University, www.rice.edu)

- Using an 8.5 × 11–inch sheet of paper, create an ad for a movie, design a house, make an object better, illustrate an ad for an object. (Tufts University, www.tufts.edu)

- Create a short story using one of the following topics:

  1. The End of MTV

  2. Confessions of a Middle-School Bully

  3. The Professor Disappeared

  4. The Mysterious Lab

     (Tufts University, www.tufts.edu)

- If you had a full day with no commitments, no homework, no home responsibilities, and only the money in your pocket, what would you do? Where would you go? Whom would you take with you? You can use whatever space and medium desired. (Johns Hopkins University, www.jhu.edu)

- You have just completed your 300-page autobiography. Please submit page 217. (University of Pennsylvania, www.upenn.edu)

© JIST Works

IT'S YOUR TURN

Think about what you'd most enjoy sharing with us creatively (video, audio, watercolor, ink drawings, cartoons, poster, book cover) and describe what you would do—and the "story" you'd be telling through this vehicle. Jot down your preliminary ideas.

_____

_____

_____

_____

_____

_____

Writing Samples

- Writing sample. Please submit a copy of a graded research, expository, or creative paper (in the English language) with instructor's comments. The paper should be one that you have written recently. (Reed College, www.reed.edu)

- The Committee on Admission is interested in getting to know each candidate as well as possible through the application process. The following essay question is designed to demonstrate your writing skills and facilitate our full appreciation of who you are. Attach your response on separate sheets. The quality of Rice's academic, cultural, and social life is heavily influenced by the unique life experiences and cultural traditions each student brings. What perspectives do you feel that you will contribute to life at Rice? Most applicants are able to respond successfully in two to three double-spaced pages. (Rice University, www.rice.edu)

- Please send a copy of an analytical paper you submitted for an English or History class (such as a critical analysis of a work of literature, film, music, or art). This sample must show your teacher's comments and/or grade. Creative writing samples and essays written in class are not acceptable for this requirement. (Sarah Lawrence College, www.slc.edu)

- Please send us one example of expository prose that you have written for a school assignment. Describe the assignment on a sheet of paper and attach a photocopy of the original, complete with the teacher's comments and grade. You should submit an analytical essay, a book review, or a research paper (short stories, poetry, plays, or lab reports are not expository prose). No limits are placed on length, but we suggest that your submission be of at least two typewritten pages. (Hamilton College, www.hamilton.edu)

IT'S YOUR TURN

Decide how you'd like to creatively write your story—a poem? A play? A print advertisement? What would your message be? Jot down your preliminary ideas here.

_____

_____

_____

_____

_____

_____

Interest in a Particular University

- Write an essay of no more than 500 words indicating what most influenced you to apply to The George Washington University. (www.gwu.edu)

- Students choose to attend Knox based on many factors, including our academic reputation, distinguished faculty, intimate class sizes, and diverse campus community, as well as the success of our graduates. How did you become interested in Knox and why do you think Knox might be a good match for you? (Knox College, www.knox.edu)

- What is there about you—your values, goals, interests, experiences, talents, style—that makes a good match with Kenyon? Why are you attracted to Kenyon? What do you want the Admissions Committee to know about you? (Kenyon College, www.kenyon.edu)

© JIST Works

- What attracts you to our college? Why do you want to become an undergraduate student here?

- The core mission of the University of San Francisco is to promote learning in the Jesuit Catholic tradition so that students acquire the knowledge, skills, values, and sensitivities they need to succeed as persons, professionals, and architects of a more humane and just world. Please compose a one- or two-page essay about yourself that tells us how you will help the University to carry out its mission. (University of San Francisco, www.usfca.edu)

- Please tell us what you find distinctive about Grinnell and why you are applying (limited to 700 characters). (Grinnell College, www.grinnell.edu)

- Give your personal background, describe

  a. How you would contribute to fostering diversity and inclusion in the Whitman community or

  b. An encounter that demonstrated the importance of diversity to you.

  (Whitman College, www.whitman.edu)

- There are thousands of U.S. colleges and universities. Why is Occidental on your college list? What distinguishes it from the other schools that you are considering? (Occidental College, www.oxy.edu)

- Your personal statement should indicate your interest in Illinois State and explain circumstances that may affect our admission decision and that are not readily apparent from academic records. (Illinois State University, www.ilstu.edu)

- Bowdoin is a liberal-arts college which is unusually vibrant intellectually. Some students enter Bowdoin with a clear commitment to a particular course of study; others come considering a broader range of academic possibilities while seeking the intellectual path which most excites them. What all students will share is exposure to the breadth and depth the Bowdoin curriculum provides. Describe what you expect your academic journey at Bowdoin to include. (Bowdoin College, www.bowdoin.edu)

- Why did you become interested in our college?

- UVM values a diverse student body. What contributions might you make to our campus community outside of academic achievement? (University of Vermont, www.uvm.edu)

- "Why Reed?" essay. How did you first become interested in Reed, and why do you think Reed would be an appropriate place, both academically and socially, to continue your education? This essay is instrumental in helping the admission committee determine the match between you and Reed, so please be thorough. (Reed College, www.reed.edu)

It's Your Turn

Tell us why you want to be here. Envision your first week or two—or even junior year—on campus. What will you be doing? Jot down your preliminary ideas here.

_____

_____

_____

_____

_____

Self-Expression

- Self-identity and personal expression take many forms. Music, food, art, and clothing can make a statement. Politics, religion, nationality, and ethnicity often act as defining attributes. Colored wristbands and blogs express opinions and viewpoints while the minutia that adorns a refrigerator or a notebook can be clues to someone's passions. Are you an oldest child? Do you surf? Are you a vegetarian? Did you wear flip-flops to the prom? Do you have a tattoo? Who are *you*? (Tufts University, www.tufts.edu)

- Write in 300 words (or less) page 256 of your autobiography from the perspective of old age. (Furman University, www.furman.edu)

© JIST Works

- In three to five sentences, please tell us what makes you unique. (Gonzaga University, www.gonzaga.edu)

IT's YOUR TURN

An open-ended question: What do you truly wish you could tell an admissions dean if you could say anything at all about yourself? Jot down your preliminary ideas here.

_____

_____

_____

_____

_____

_____

General Accomplishment or Interest

- Lafayette considers all applicants who are U.S. citizens or permanent residents for our academic scholarships. In an effort to learn more about you, we ask that you describe an intellectual or creative interest or accomplishment. (Lafayette College, www.lafayette.edu)

- Are there activities you did not do in secondary school but might try at Kenyon? (Kenyon College, www.kenyon.edu)

- Describe one thing you haven't yet accomplished in your life that you really want to do. Explain how being at Syracuse will help you accomplish it. (Syracuse University, www.syr.edu)

- Is there anything—whether it be politics, science, languages, culture, or anything at all—that you are particularly passionate about? What is it and how did you become inspired to pursue it? How have you been involved in following this interest? Do you have any idea where you'd like to take it in the future? (University of Richmond, www.ur.edu)

- Do you have a tentative (or firm) career plan (or dream)? Please describe it. (Carleton College, www.carleton.edu)

It's Your Turn

What about your life so far has been the most rewarding? Can it be quantified with an award? Is it something you "just know" about yourself? How does this accomplishment make you feel? Jot down your preliminary ideas here.

_____

_____

_____

_____

_____

_____

Unique Opportunities or Obstacles

- What opportunities have you sought that went beyond what was offered to every student at your school or what circumstances have you overcome in order to achieve what you have? Of what are you most proud? (University of Richmond, www.ur.edu)

- Are there any unique circumstances you'd like to discuss which may have had some bearing on your academic performance?

- A high school curriculum does not always afford much intellectual freedom. Describe one of your unsatisfied intellectual passions. How might you apply this interest to serve the common good and make a difference in society? (Tufts University, www.tufts.edu)

It's Your Turn

If you have faced and successfully overcome (or are in the process of overcoming) a particular challenge, is this something we would want to know about you? Does it help to define your character and make you who you are? Jot down your preliminary ideas here.

_____

_____

© JIST Works

_____

_____

_____

_____

Additional Questions

- If you have participated in any significant research activity outside of school, please provide a brief description and limit this response to one or two paragraphs. (Optional for all applicants, Duke University, www.duke.edu)

- How will your individual background, experiences, and personal identity influence your educational pursuits and your contributions to the campus community at the University of Florida? (www.ufl.edu)

- We seek to understand and appreciate you as an individual. If there is a parent, sibling, other relative, or friend of yours who you think could help us do that, we would be happy to receive a one-page letter from one of them. This optional information will be considered in our understanding of you as a person, but will not be formally evaluated as part of your application. (Optional for all applicants, Duke University, www.duke.edu)

- What would you pursue, design, or accomplish if money were no object? (Colgate University, www.colgate.edu)

- What is the one question you wish we had asked you to respond to in your essay?

- What fictional character or characters from literature, film, theatre, or television have intrigued you or taught you something and why? (Barnard College, www.barnard.columbia.edu)

- Write a concise statement with any additional information that is important to convey to the admissions committee. Information that may be important might include your aspirations, work experience, creative talents, factors affecting your academic record, or why you are applying to the University of Wisconsin. (University of Wisconsin, www.wisc.edu)

- Tell us what you like to do for fun. (University of Pennsylvania, www.upenn.edu)

- What criterion (criteria) do you consider to be the most important in deciding the college you will attend?

- [About a teacher] He/she has influenced me because…. (Carleton College, www.carleton.edu)

- In three to five sentences, please tell us about someone you admire. (Gonzaga University, www.gonzaga.edu)

- Colleges, like people, have personalities and characteristics. Dickinson was founded for high purposes: to educate students in the "useful" arts and sciences through interaction with the world, so that they might become leaders and true citizens of the world. Describe your specific goals, and—using what you know about Dickinson's distinctive character, top programs, and campus environment—describe how Dickinson will facilitate the fulfillment of those goals, as well as how your personality and character will fit with Dickinson's. (Dickinson College, www.dickinson.edu)

- An American adage states that "curiosity killed the cat." If that is correct, why do we celebrate people like Galileo, Lincoln, and Gandhi, individuals who thought about longstanding problems in new ways or who defied conventional thinking to achieve great results? (Tufts University, www.tufts.edu)

- History's great events often turn on small moments. For example, what if Rosa Parks had given up her seat on that Montgomery bus in 1955? What if Pope John Paul I had not died in 1978 after a month in office? What if Gore had beaten Bush in Florida and won the 2000 U.S. Presidential election? Using your knowledge of American or world history, choose a defining moment and imagine an alternative historical scenario if that key event had played out differently. (Tufts University, www.tufts.edu)

- Please react to the following quote from Christopher Morley (1890–1957, American author): "Read, every day, something no one else is reading. Think, every day, something no one else is thinking. Do, every day, something no one else would be silly enough to do. It is bad for the mind to continually be part of unanimity." (University of Richmond, www.ur.edu)

© JIST Works

Specialty Applications

In addition to the broad range of possible questions discussed on the preceding pages, some schools require special applications for various programs or schools within the college.

Here are some typical examples of the questions you can expect for various supplements.

Athletic Supplement

The Common Application Athletic Supplement® (www.commonapp.org/common2007_AddlForms.pdf) requires you to specify team sports you played that are important to you. You are required to provide the name of the sport, years played (by grade: 9, 10, 11, 12), JV and/or varsity letters earned, event or position, whether you were captain, and usually the coach's name for each sport. In addition, you are encouraged to list times, records, and awards. Height and weight information is considered optional.

Arts Supplement

Students applying to schools for admission into an arts program are generally asked to provide a portfolio that reflects their range of work or a CD or audiotape that depicts their performance. For instance, Carnegie Mellon University requires students applying to the Schools of Architecture, Art, Design, Drama, or Music within the College of Fine Arts to register for an audition or portfolio review.

> **Note:** You should provide copies of any material submitted (for instance, CD, DVD, audiotape, photocopies of artwork, and so on) and should not expect that the college will return these materials.

The Common Application Arts Supplement® (www.commonapp.org/common2007_AddlForms.pdf) requires you to specify your arts medium (for instance, if you are a prospective music major and instrumentalist, specify your instrument; likewise, based on your expertise and interest, you might instead indicate voice, composition, world music tradition, songwriting; theater and dance; or visual arts and film as your medium).

In addition, the instructions stipulate the following:

- Have an instructor who is familiar with your work send us a letter of recommendation.

- Enclose a 10-minute CD or DVD demonstrating contrasting examples of expression and technique.

- Include a list of what is on the CD or DVD. (Do not submit videotapes; do not submit audiotapes of chorus.)

- FOR MUSIC: Attach a resume to the supplemental form that summarizes experience with instrument(s), voice, and/or composition, giving years studied, name(s) of teacher(s) or group(s), repertoire, and awards/honors received.

- FOR THEATER/DANCE: Attach a resume to the supplemental form that summarizes experience, giving years studied, name(s) of teacher(s) or group(s), repertoire, special programs, and awards/honors received.

- FOR VISUAL ARTS/FILM: Attach a resume to the supplemental form that summarizes experience, giving dates, institutions or programs, and awards/honors received. Include a brief description of each course or workshop attended, and describe any related experiences.

Honors Program Application

Some colleges offer prospective freshmen the opportunity to apply to an honors college within the university. For many, a supplemental application is required. For instance, the following questions are asked on the Simmons College honors program supplemental application; www.simmons.edu. In addition to submitting an original graded paper, applicants are asked to answer either of two essay questions:

1. The Honors Program encourages students to experience life in another country. If you were to study abroad for a month or a semester, what country would you prefer to visit and what would you hope to learn from your experiences in another culture?

2. Honors students at Simmons often take an active role in student government and organizations, including our student newspaper, *The Simmons Voice*. Write the lead editorial for the *Voice* on an issue of local, national, or global importance.

© JIST Works

Advice from Your (Former) Peers

It's often said that misery loves company. In the spirit of that (but with an optimistic twist), this next section presents the aspects of essay writing that the students profiled in chapter 7 of this book found most challenging. You will also find many additional recommendations to help *you* move past writer's block on your way to a well-crafted essay.

The Hardest Part About Writing My Essay

- "Being succinct. I found there was so much I wanted to say about myself and so many ways that I wanted to show who I am that it became difficult to keep it to the required word count. To solve this I simply narrowed my focus. I actually narrowed it a lot. I focused on one hour of my life that I felt showed a few different things about me. I wasn't thrilled with my essay but felt it was an interesting read and would stand out in an admissions officer's mind." (Chelsea M., Wake Forest University)

- "The hardest part about writing the essay was actually sitting down and getting it done. A solution to this would possibly be to write bits and pieces each day. Get thoughts down when they come to you, instead of trying to pull an entire essay out of nowhere." (Jeff F., Marist College)

- "First, it was finding a topic. We did a preliminary thing in drama class since many of us requested we do one. So after going through that list with my parents, we decided upon my bike trip. I always have a hard time starting since I'm a terrible procrastinator, but once I had it done, the revisions went much easier." (Meg A., Knox College)

- "Choosing a topic was the most difficult part of writing my college essay. While I was always instructed to write about something mean-ingful in my life, I was also encouraged to write about something unique, something that might not be a common essay topic. I found it very challenging to pick the topic that would best reveal my experi-ences and characteristics—who I really am—which would at the same time be interesting and distinct. (For example, I have gone on the Appalachia trip for a number of years, and the trip is one of the most important things in my life; however, as one of my teachers shared with me, more and more students are writing on topics like that, so I might better share myself by writing on a different topic, despite Appalachia's significance in my life.)" (Katharine C., Mount Holyoke College)

- "As I said before, the actual act of starting to write was very difficult. After that, the next hardest part was knowing where the line is between trying to show the essay readers who I am and being too chummy. I really didn't want to sound like I was trying to rub elbows with the reader, but I did want the essay to sound personal. Eventually, I just decided to kind of stick to the bare bones of the essay, but write it in such a way that sounded like the way I talk. This way I could portray my personality and style while answering what the essay asked for." (Caitlin S., Rensselaer Polytechnic Institute)

- "I am known as a huge procrastinator and the toughest part for me was motivating myself to do it. I only needed to compose one essay for all my applications, yet I still managed to wait until late November to write it." (Jayson N., University of Maine–Orono)

- "The hardest part about writing my essay was staying concise, modifying it, and keeping it to the word limit. I had to sacrifice things I liked without compromising the purpose and detail of the essay." (Camila G., Duke University)

- "The hardest part about writing the essay was probably just answering the question completely. Although it was a fairly simple essay and I don't have trouble with writing, the weight of this one essay was enough to make me nervous about writing an essay of any kind." (Brian W., Dickinson College)

- "Definitely the topic. Things about ourselves seem mundane to us, but thinking of how these are interesting and telling is a stretch. Something I do every day—running—turned out to be the perfect topic." (Brandon C., University of Richmond)

- "Probably the most difficult part of writing a college essay is getting started. In many instances there might be several topics that an applicant can write about to sufficiently fulfill the college essay requirement, but I wanted to find not just the best one, but also the 'right' one. Once I selected a topic and sketched out some points that I wanted to cover in my essay, the writing flowed easier. I would sometimes find myself hung up on trying to gear my writing more towards what I thought the college admissions office wanted to read instead of just telling my story. Once you get away from that, the writing will be easier to write and better to read." (Marc G., Worcester Polytechnic Institute)

© JIST Works

- "Writing something unique and captivating—without going too far." (Matt K., The Ohio State University)

- "The hardest part was writing on the topic I had chosen. I wrote about a personal fear that I had and how I fought through it. It was definitely difficult to write about something that close to me, but in the end I felt that the subject I had chosen allowed me to write a meaningful essay that thoroughly represented my attributes." (Shelley P., Tulane University and University of Connecticut)

- "The pressure of having to write the essay! Having to convey everything I wanted the university to know about me into one 500-word essay. I also wanted the essay to reflect my writing style and personality as a person, which is hard to do when you're writing to such a formal and serious audience." (Stephanie C., Fordham University)

Additional Recommendations for Writing a Great Application Essay

- "Don't wait until the last minute. Absolutely don't put it off, especially if you're dreading it. I like writing and still dreaded the essay portion and put it off until the last minute (literally I mailed three applications the day they were due to be postmarked by) and regretted that I didn't have more time. Also, don't start too soon. The truth is that one always evolves as a writer and it is very unlikely that the final essay to be sent to schools in November would be one someone wrote as a sophomore in high school. Junior and senior years are very demanding academically. When a student fills a day with classes, sports practice, club meetings, and a part-time job, it's hard to finish school work, let alone college applications and essays. It's going to be stressful regardless, but by starting to brainstorm junior year and focus on writing the summer before senior year, one diminishes stress a bit." (Chelsea M., Wake Forest University)

- "Start writing your junior year, not to have *the* essay, but just to start writing about yourself and bouncing ideas around. In my English class junior year, we had a year-long project where we wrote personal essays and compiled them into a booklet at the end of the year. It was helpful, because we got a chance to write creatively, and practice self-reflection and self-expression. I didn't use any of those essays for my college essay, but it definitely started my thought process." (Julia H., Vassar College)

- "I would say if you are not working on it in a class, that you should set deadlines for yourself. I am certainly not one of those people who sets dates and is able to keep them—heck, I don't even have a day planner—but the fact that I did my essay as a part of my UConn English class made me stick to a schedule and allowed ample time for review. Really, the important thing is that you go through a review process. If I have learned one thing taking humanities classes, I have learned that typing the last sentence is *not* the end of the paper. If you don't review and revise, even if it's only a quick once-over, you're selling yourself short." (David S., George Washington University)

- "Begin early and write about something that matters to you, even if it does not seem 'collegey.' For instance, one of my friends wrote about comic books and I wrote mine on how much I like libraries. People tend to respond best if you are sincere. Do it when you do not have something else to stress about. Life is a bit easier that way. The most important thing is to just push through it and don't get discouraged. Once you start working on everything, it is not nearly as hard as it seems." (Britt M., Grinnell College)

- "My college had the essay be optional but I think it makes a difference. They used the application for admission to help determine scholarship money and I know that the essay helped me to get a scholarship. I used the same essay on several local scholarship applications as my writing sample. I did receive one of these scholarships for students going into education. I found that when I was working on my essay it was good to take a break for a few hours and then go back and reread it to make sure it made logical sense. Things that look okay when you are working sometimes don't make sense when you read it later." (Jason C., Concordia University Chicago)

- "Always organize your thoughts and have other people proofread your work. What you don't notice that may not flow well, someone else who reads it will." (Brett W., Rochester Institute of Technology)

- "The earlier you start writing the better. It's important to have the time to consult with your teachers, who will be more than happy to critique your essay for you, while not burdening them at the last minute. Additionally, you will remove pressure from yourself by finishing your application early." (Kyle M., Lafayette College)

- "I would like to suggest that a good amount of time should be taken on planning the structure and meaning of the essay, an hour or two writing it initially, and then a number of hours spread out over time

© JIST Works

to revise and perfect the essay. Of course, this revision process takes a while, so I suggest that beginning the essay junior year will ultimately create the best essay in time to send to colleges in their senior year." (Don R., Fairfield University)

- "The best place to start is the common application. Almost all the essays on the common app can be tailored to answer other questions in other applications. They are really general and give the writer an opportunity to choose a topic that is meaningful or shows something about his or her character. For this reason, students should view the essay as a tool. The essay should not only illustrate the student's writing abilities, but show something unique about the student that a reader could not gather from the lists of extracurricular activities and achievements or lists of courses taken. It is also important when writing responses to questions, that an applicant keep an open mind. I mean that one shouldn't choose one topic 'because it would be an impressive story' but try a few. I must have written (or at least started) 30 different essays. In the end I simply chose the one I 'hated least' that accomplished what I had wanted to accomplish. My biggest piece of advice to an applicant is to be different. Don't try too hard to be different, but show something unique and relatable by another reader. Tell a story or make the essay move in some way. Instead of telling a reader what you're like, *show* them. And most importantly, be grammatically correct." (Chelsea M., Wake Forest University)

- "Don't write something you don't believe in or try to portray yourself differently than you normally would. If you write what you believe, chances are you will sound more forceful and confident about what you say. The main goal of the college essay is to give your prospective college an idea of just who you are and whether or not you are a good fit for the school—in 500 words or less, usually. The more novel or interesting your method of doing this, the better." (Nicholas M., Tufts University)

When Is the Best Time to Write Your Application Essay?

With only a few exceptions, the majority of admission experts and college students polled suggested that the summer immediately following the junior year of high school is the optimal time for writing essays. You can always further revise, modify, and polish the essays during the first few months of senior year.

- "It's good to brainstorm and maybe make an outline before school starts, but I think better writing happens when you are engaged at school; you are also given availability of the teachers and the guidance of others." (Matthew P., University of Maryland–Baltimore County)

- "My sophomore English teacher and National Honor Society leader held writing workshops specifically for composing your college essays. Here, I was given the information about writing the proper college essay. Always stick to the topic. Short, sweet, and to the point (to a certain degree) will most likely lead to a successful essay (you need to remember that they have countless applications to read through). Personalize your essay (make it memorable)." (Jayson N., University of Maine–Orono)

- "Some good advice I got was to be creative, and write what you know. The 'be creative' part was from my friend, whose mother had been on the admissions panel, and from the school guidance counselors, who talked about this one person getting into their college with an application essay about chocolate. The write-what-you-know part was from a professional writer whose novels I adore. She sometimes posts writing advice on her live journal." (Kelsey M., Worcester Polytechnic Institute)

- "It can be hard to sit down and write a college essay before senior year has even started, but senior year can be quite hectic with sports or jobs in addition to school and homework. Simply writing down ideas about themes or main points to be incorporated into your essay will serve as a great jumping-off point when it comes time to write the actual draft." (Ali M., Stetson University)

- "I started writing my essays in October/November. I was able to bring my essay to Thanksgiving dinner, where I had the luxury of having a family of former newspaper editors look over my essay. I feel I began at a good time, after I had settled into my senior year. I would recommend timing out the essay writing in a block where you could work on it continuously, not in a choppy manner. Work around your schoolwork and give enough time to think out your essay." (Meghan H., James Madison University)

- "My English teacher junior year always emphasized 'show don't tell' and told me to incorporate my own voice into my essays. As a result

© JIST Works

I wrote candidly and honestly. My writing was very revealing of who I am." (Camila G., Duke University)

- "Start thinking about the essay during the summer, but don't stress about writing it until you're really working on applications. People get all worked up. Once you're in college, you'll forget how hard it was to go through the application process. Make it as painless as you have to. Don't wait too long to begin, but don't freak out if everyone else has started writing during their junior year. Plus, if you begin writing it too early, it won't sound like you. Everyone does a lot of changing senior year. You will be at least somewhat different from the summer to the time applications are due." (Vickie A., University of Richmond)

- "Make sure you aren't rushed at the time when all of your applications are due. Allow yourself enough time to proofread and make it your absolute best work." (Lindsey W., University of Connecticut)

- "Have many people read your essay and give you feedback. If you have a clever essay (such as mine), you're probably just going to get, 'Wow, that's great!' because it's so different. Push people to point out any weak spots. Don't feel the need to take everyone's opinion into account, though. If you don't agree with it, feel free to not include it. It's your essay, after all. As I said before, make sure that your personality shows through! That is, above all, the most important part. Show the admissions board what makes you tick. Convince them that their school cannot afford to pass up such a wonderful individual. You are selling yourself through this essay. Treat it like an advertisement. You don't want to sell anything false to the consumer, but you want to show only the best sides of yourself. If you have less-than-stellar grades or SAT scores, it's the essay that will really convince the board that they need you." (Vickie A., University of Richmond)

- "I started off just jotting down notes the summer after my junior year so that when it came time to write my essay senior year, I knew what I wanted to say." (Megan S., Furman University)

- "The timing is important to have everything ready in time but it is also important to be mentally ready to write the essays, have a construction in mind—not just writing for the writing's sake. Give yourself at least a week to think about the topic, another week to write it, and then another week to improve it." (Veronika H., Wesleyan University)

- "I would say don't start too early because then you might experience something that is better to write about, but don't wait too long either because then the process will be rushed and probably not the best essay you could write." (Jamie H., Dickinson College)

- "I think the summer before senior year or the fall of senior year are the prime essay-writing times. You've had lots of experiences and chances are there are some interesting stories to tell about yourself. Plan a few weeks for the essay, though. Reflection takes time and creativity springs forth erratically." (Brandon C., University of Richmond)

- "The essay may be important but it is important to remember that it is all the factors together that make a student a good candidate for acceptance—grades, extracurricular activities, leadership skills, work ethic. However, the essay is helpful to show certain characteristics about oneself that may make one more appealing to the admissions staff (for example, writing about overcoming a challenge or dealing with adversity, etc.). Applying to colleges is a stressful time and it helps to find one school that is almost a guaranteed acceptance to help take the pressure off." (Amy W., Siena College)

Key Points: Chapter 5

- The Common Application makes it very easy to apply to multiple institutions. Keep in mind that you'll need, at minimum, one personal essay as well as one short-answer question response. Know whether your target institutions require supplemental applications.

- Consider the range of essay questions asked by many different colleges—and not just the ones you are targeting. From the sampling in this chapter to those you can easily research on the Internet, you'll find many good starting places.

- If you are seeking to pursue a sport, a musical interest, another performing art, architectural studies, one of the fine studio arts, or perhaps even engineering or technology studies in college, you will quite possibly be asked to complete a supplemental college application that includes a few key examples of your work in your field of interest.

- Peer-level advice from students who have gone through the application process successfully can take some of the mystery out of the essay-writing process and empower you with salient recommendations that are specific and well-tested.

© JIST Works

Chapter 6

Other Pieces of the College Application Package

This book is devoted to writing a great college application essay. But as you know, the essay is just one of the components of an application package. This chapter gives details on all the other components of a college application, starting with the essentials and then touching on some extra things you may or may not be asked to provide.

The Essentials

Ranked in order of what is typically most important, here are the elements generally required in a college application package. Some schools weight several items equally (in other words, a college might say that the transcript, SAT scores, and class rank all are ranked #1 as the most important items in a candidate's application). Of course, not all schools require all of these items. A brief description of each item follows with advice from university admissions experts from around the country where applicable.

High School Transcript

The student's high school transcript almost universally is ranked by admissions deans as the #1 criterion considered in a candidate's application package.

Most high school guidance offices provide seniors with forms used to specifically request that copies of transcripts be forwarded to certain colleges or universities. Schools will also generally advise making requests several weeks before deadlines; advance notice is always preferred.

High schools also provide information to colleges detailing rigor of the high school curriculum, course offerings available to students (for instance, number of AP [advanced placement] classes), and class rank. Admissions offices view a student's transcript from the standpoint of academic achievement in core academic classes (social studies, history, English, mathematics, science, and foreign language[s]).

Achievement in the specials—physical education, health, performing arts (chorus, band, painting, theater, sculpture, and so on), computer and business classes, and others—is typically not taken into account. Of course, the admissions offices at colleges will *see* these grades and a student earning all *A*s in specials looks more well-rounded than one who performs poorly in these choices. There are, of course, exceptions. Students pursuing admittance to an arts school will certainly want to present strong achievement in all of the arts. The typical GPA considered by a comprehensive or liberal-arts university would not prevail.

Tip: *Check with your high school guidance office to see a sample of how a transcript is presented. In most instances, schools show only final grades in each class for each of the first three years in high school. In other words, if you had several poor grades the first few semesters of your freshman year but pulled up achievement for the final two semesters to end a class with a "B," a D+ in one semester probably won't show up on the transcript.*

If your transcript does reveal any weak areas in academics, you might want to consider addressing this in your application and, possibly, essay. Admissions offices tend to be a bit more forgiving of a sluggish start to a high school career provided that your performance tracks consistently upward by your junior year. But if your transcript is spotty throughout all three years, some explanation might be in order.

If your transcript reflects that you have consistently taken classes at the highest level (for instance, your high school offers A, B, and C levels for all academic courses and you have always taken the highest A-level classes), the fact that you persevered and stayed in these more demanding courses despite perhaps earning *C*s in a few will mean more than opting out to C-level classes in which you earned *A*s. Likewise, if you have consistently advanced through a subject area, challenging yourself with higher-level offerings, but couldn't always earn *A*s, this will also be evaluated in a more positive light than someone who takes random courses, no advanced coursework within a field, and does earn the *A*s.

A classic example is the student who has had a year or two of foreign language in middle school. Let's say you studied French in 7th and 8th grade.

© JIST Works

For freshman year, you probably started off with French II. If you continue along the expected track, by senior year, you should be starting with French V. Provided that your performance is at least reasonably good, this will serve you much better than if you took French II freshman year, and then switched to Spanish I your sophomore year, and then dropped foreign language altogether by your junior year.

Academic Progress Report

You will generally be asked to have your high school report your current grades at the time you are completing the application—usually the grades posted for the first semester of your senior year—as soon as they are available. Colleges want to see these updated grades to make sure you haven't slacked off since the end of your junior year. Senior slide is something to guard against. Despite wanting to enjoy your senior year, you really still need to keep your eye on the ball and do your best to continue the level of achievement you've established by junior year.

Standardized Test Scores (SAT and/or ACT)

These scores are considered anywhere from #2 to #5 in importance according to admissions experts, depending on the institution. Although the trend over recent years has been for more colleges to require standardized test scores, there is a move afloat by some institutions to abandon them altogether. Traditionally, SAT scores were most commonly accepted (and, frequently, required) by institutions in the Northeast and along the Eastern Seaboard; ACT scores were much more popular than SATs in the Midwest, for instance. Many institutions today that require standardized test scores will accept either (or both).

Unless you are absolutely sure of the schools you will actually apply to—and have researched exactly what they require in terms of testing—your best bet would be to take each test at least once. More details about the SAT and ACT appear in chapter 1.

SAT Subject Test Scores can be as important as #2 in the ranking for schools that require them to #6; many schools do not require them at all. Generally, the more competitive institutions ask for up to two SAT Subject Tests in different subject areas (for example, you will not be able to take Mathematics Level 1 *and* Mathematics Level 2); in some instances, the college may waive the requirement for the SAT Subject Test scores if you take the ACT with the writing test.

Strength of Academic Curriculum

For all schools for which this is considered, it is consistently ranked #1 (along with the student transcript). For many schools, this includes the equally important criterion of Number of AP Classes—both the number offered in a school *and* the number you've taken. For instance, some very small high schools may offer only a handful of AP classes, but the student took nearly all; in other cases, a large, affluent public high school may offer dozens of options, but the student opted to take one AP class or none. Jean Jordan, Interim Dean of Admission, Emory University, states:

Note: *At the time this book was researched, no schools interviewed were yet considering the results of the writing portion of the SAT Reasoning Test. The Writing section was introduced to the longstanding Mathematics and Critical Reading (formerly Verbal) sections of the SAT several years ago. Most admissions officers indicate that it is simply too soon to begin evaluating how the Writing component will be used in evaluating student applications.*

> *Curriculum is much more important than GPA. How rigorous is the high school's curriculum? How challenging a program has the student pursued? This, along with the essay and rest of the application, has a big impact on us. We look for students who are involved on campus and will contribute to Emory. We try to assess how much this student gives to their school environment and their community.*

Rank in Senior Class

The majority of schools for which this criterion is important rank it at #1, along with transcripts, test scores, and strength of curriculum. Other schools place this second or third on the list of important criteria considered.

GPA

GPA (Grade Point Average) is nearly always considered #1 or #2 in importance among the other factors. Regardless of how a high school might calculate GPA, a college typically converts the numbers on the transcript to a 4.0 scale, with an *A* earning a 4, a *B* earning a 3, and so on. GPA is usually considered only on pure academic subjects (as noted earlier, "specials" are generally not calculated). GPA is one criterion used to compare students with one another.

© JIST Works

The Application Essay

Throughout this book, you will find significant input regarding the value and importance of the application essay. Depending on the school, the essay can rank as high as #3 (right after transcript and scores) to #7 in importance when weighing a candidate's application.

Don Bishop, Associate Vice President for Enrollment Management at Creighton University, notes:

> *Creighton also reviews application essays for merit consideration. We review about 4,200 applications and provide merit awards of $5,000 or more to only about 50 percent of the admitted applicant pool. The essay is part of this process.*

Douglas Christiansen, Ph.D., Associate Provost for Enrollment and Dean of Admissions, Vanderbilt University, states:

> *We use the college essay to help us better learn about the student. We are seeking the student who is ethical and upfront with good analytical abilities. We want someone who is creative and service-oriented and who displays an understanding of the importance of diversity. We want to develop a match and build a freshmen class with students sharing a similar value system but reflecting a wide range of thoughts and expressions.*

Paul Marthers, Dean of Admission, Reed College, states:

> *Essays are considered after the transcript (courses, grades) and standardized tests. The essay, extracurriculars, and recommendations help paint a portrait of the person behind the numbers.*

Letters of Recommendation

Letters of recommendation vary widely in importance to different schools, with some placing their importance as #2 on the list and others ranking them as low as #8. But they are a requirement of virtually all college applications.

Advice from the Experts

Gil Villanueva, Dean of Admissions, Brandeis University, says this about letters of recommendation:

Be sure to ask those who can and will portray you in a positive light and those who know you best as an individual as well as a student. There are moments when recommendations come across as mediocre or even somewhat negative. If you are interested in sending more than what the institution requires, then be certain to ask those who can represent you in another way.

Jean Jordan (Emory) states:

My biggest complaint is when I get letters from people who don't know students, but know their parents (big-name people, well-recognized). This is not nearly as effective as having someone write who knows the student well and can provide a good perspective. If a student has worked every summer at the same job and the employer knows him or her very well and speaks to their organizational ability and how they've taken on a management role, those kinds of letters can be very important.

Vince Cuseo, Dean of Admission, Occidental College, suggests:

Additional letters of recommendation can be important if a student has considerable talent in an area not covered by an academic recommendation (e.g., debate, music, internship). That said, read the directions for each college carefully. Some will encourage additional recommendations; others expressly discourage them.

Adding Up the Pieces

Jeanne Jenkins, Director, Strategic Initiatives, Admissions Office, Rensselaer Polytechnic Institute, had some insights to share about the interplay between two important pieces of the package. "We like to compare the essay with letters of recommendation. Most of the time, the pieces of an application come together in a way that seems pretty predictable. When they don't make sense, we'll make an extra phone call, read the essay again, and look at the letters of recommendation again. Often times, it is a letter of recommendation or the student essay that brings out a student's very strong interest or passion—and it might be something the high school knows nothing about. Bottom line, for the most part, when we read student recommendations and essays, it's generally clear that they are all about the same person."

© JIST Works

Richard Zeiser, Dean of Admission, University of Hartford, explains:

Everyone knows that being a member of an athletic team requires good skills in organization and time management. A letter from a coach or employer or civic group leader speaking about this same athlete's ability to also work 25 hours a week in a part-time job or volunteer with an agency can be very meaningful—in addition to that individual's academic abilities.

Don Bishop (Creighton) suggests the following:

It is helpful to hear from teachers and adults who have coached or managed the student in an activity or work environment. These letters tell us about the applicant as both a student and a school or community citizen. I even like getting a recommendation from a parent—although I understand it is highly biased. A great letter from a parent, however, does not make up for a poor essay by the student. We do not enroll parents—we enroll their students. Students need to rely on themselves more than their parents—despite this generation of helicopter parents. Parents do their kids a disservice by trying to control their student's efforts. With that said, I like hearing from the parent what they like about their child. I take it as a biased statement but it can still be helpful.

Anything the adults can tell us about the applicant that we see supported by the high school transcript, resume/list of involvements and accomplishments, and the essay and/or personal statement will reassure the admissions committee and is a positive thing. This is particularly true when we see that statements made by the students are also reiterated by the adults who are professionals.

Eric Simonelli, Admission Advisor, University of Rhode Island, added the following:

Many teachers use a grid year in and year out and just highlight facts about a specific student. However, if a student has experienced a situation that needs to be addressed, it is very useful to have these issues explained by a professional.

Dealing with Forms

In addition to the advice provided by admissions experts, you should be aware that most colleges provide a form that you will use to collect your recommendations, including those from teachers. There is a section on the form that you complete before giving the form to the teacher. Most forms include a box to check if you are waiving your right to see the recommendation letter; you should check this. Most teachers and others writing letters of recommendation on your behalf will provide you with a copy, anyway. You would not be selecting someone to write a letter on your behalf who wasn't going to write powerfully about your accomplishments, right? So you should trust that what they will say is positive.

> **Tip:** *Include an ad-dressed, stamped envelope made out to the respective school when giving your teacher/employer/coach/principal the recommendation form.*

Who Should You Ask?

To help you decide which people to ask for letters of recommendation, it is always advisable to select people who have known you for some period of time and can comment effectively on the quality of your work, your work ethic and approach, key success stories (even including how you may have overcome a challenge), and other characteristics that are uniquely you.

What to Consider When Choosing People to Write Recommendation Letters

Consider the following questions that often appear on recommendation forms; try to project how a teacher or another source might respond to these questions about you. You should choose those who know you best and would evaluate you the most objectively (and positively), thus giving strong answers.

- How long have you known the student and in what capacity?
- List key adjectives that describe the applicant.
- How would you assess the student's academic performance?
- Are there other characteristics you are in a position to evaluate (i.e., work ethic, character, classroom participation, ability to work with peers, degree of motivation, responsiveness to constructive criticism, level of academic ability, suitability for college-level learning, etc.)?
- What characteristics do you believe uniquely make up this individual?

© JIST Works

- What are this student's strengths and weaknesses?

- Does he or she work up to his or her individual level of potential?

- What other insights can you provide relative to this person's unique circumstances, background, and performance?

How Will Your Teachers Evaluate You?

There is also typically a scale that asks teachers to evaluate students on the basis of a number of criteria using the following measures:

Unable to judge on this criterion

Below Average

Average

Good/Above Average

Very Good

Excellent (top 10 percent of current class)

Outstanding (top 5 percent of current class)

One of the top few ever encountered throughout entire career

The types of categories for which teachers are asked to evaluate students include the following:

- Academic achievement
- Intellectual ability
- Growth potential
- Motivation
- Creative, original thought
- Quality of writing
- Quality of classroom participation
- Leadership
- Self-discipline
- Maturity
- Reaction to criticism
- Reaction to setbacks
- Initiative
- Independence
- Self-confidence
- Work and study habits
- Character and integrity
- Empathy and concern for others
- Overall evaluation

Student Interview

Interviews with admissions personnel can rank anywhere from #2 to #6 in importance, depending on the school. Eric Simonelli (University of Rhode Island) says

> *The 2006–2007 year was the first year that URI required an essay. With more than 14,000 applications in a given year, it is being used in place of the formal interview.*

Thus, URI is placing a higher importance on the application essay, second only to the transcript and academic information.

Some schools strongly encourage students to have interviews if at all possible—and will make it more convenient for them by asking alumni who reside in a student's area to conduct the interview on behalf of the admissions office.

Try to schedule an on-campus interview with colleges that strongly interest you. This can help to strengthen your application as a prospective student. Admissions offices pay close attention to the number of contacts (visits, letters, interviews, and so on) that students have, sometimes giving greater weight to those students who show the most interest as evidenced by these activities.

Extra Credit

In addition to the basics that most colleges require, there are a few extras that may be asked for, or that you can add to give yourself an extra edge. A few points to keep in mind: Always follow the directions and provide everything that is requested. If, for instance, an application states "provide only up to two letters of recommendation," do not exceed that number. Do not omit anything that is required. Do feel free, however, to consider including some of these "extra-credit" items if they will help to strengthen your candidacy as a prospective student.

Parent-Peer Evaluations

Some schools have an actual form for this response; in other instances, schools indicate that it is acceptable to include evaluations of this type. For instance, Mount Holyoke College offers the option for a parent or peer to write a "candid appraisal of the applicant, which will help us in our task of selecting students from many highly qualified applicants to Mount

Holyoke College. We seek evidence of character, integrity, maturity, independence, strong interests, and unique abilities or qualities. We encourage you to use specific examples of experiences that may have shaped your feelings toward the applicant." (Mount Holyoke College Common Application Supplement, www.mtholyoke.edu)

Work Samples and Portfolio

Work samples and portfolios are requested where appropriate, often for academic pursuits in the arts, graphic design, architecture, and similar creative disciplines. Simply put: Follow the directions provided carefully.

Student Resume

Many admissions experts believe that the student resume is a welcome addition to the application package. The resume can rank as high as #2 among the criteria considered in the application package and as low as #9.

Notes Don Bishop (Creighton), "I like resumes—they provide an organized list of activities and interests. It is good practice for the job search process in four years."

Eric Simonelli (University of Rhode Island) states, "It is helpful in knowing what activities a student has been involved in and what he or she has accomplished outside the classroom. Here at URI, we're looking for involved students that can make a difference in the community as well as the classroom."

Vince Cuseo (Occidental) had a different opinion: "These are rarely valuable. An application may not allow enough space and freedom, but there shouldn't be many high school seniors who have done so much that a college application can't accommodate [this experience]."

Paul Marthers (Reed) advises keeping the resume under two pages.

Doug Christiansen (Vanderbilt) cautions: "Don't turn the application into a portfolio or scrapbook (unless that is what is requested). Achieve a balance, turning in what is requested and nothing more."

Jean Jordan (Emory) reminds students, "Resumes are fine as long as students don't use them in lieu of the application. The rule of thumb to remember is if what you are submitting will fit in an 8.5" × 11" file folder, feel free to include it if you believe it will augment your application. Anything larger (unless specifically requested) is not advised."

The following listing details the types of information that are often included on a resume. Usually you will find that the majority of this information fits nicely into the application form itself. But some of these distinctions might be better presented in a resume or reflected in a letter you attach to your application. Use this as a checklist to ensure that you consider any highlight or activity in any of these categories:

Academic Achievements and Honors	❏
Extracurricular Activities	❏
Music	❏
Sports	❏
Art	❏
Performing Arts	❏
Dance	❏
Other	❏
Recognition and Awards (outside academic)	❏
School Clubs	❏
Honor Society	❏
Leadership (Student Government)	❏
Foreign Language	❏
Other	❏
Volunteerism and Community Service	❏
External Club Activities	❏
Scouting	❏
Running or Ski Clubs (outside school)	❏
Internship Experiences (formal or informal)	❏
Mentoring or Shadowing Experiences	❏
Work/Employment History (part-time jobs)	❏
Special Skills	❏
Foreign Languages	❏
PC Skills	❏
Other	❏

© JIST Works

Personal Statement

When a personal statement is required on an application (or application supplement), follow the directions carefully. If the application does not require a personal statement, you should not add it to the package.

Extracurricular Activities

Schools differ widely in how extracurricular activities are evaluated, ranking from #2 in importance to #10. Virtually all admissions experts remind students that the important thing with extracurricular activities is to show depth of interest and involvement and not breadth. In other words, long-term, committed membership in one or two organizations, clubs, and/or sports with real contributions, leadership positions, and so on is much more meaningful than a smattering of clubs and activities in which the student participated just a half-year.

Volunteerism/Community Service

As with extracurriculars, deep involvement with just a few programs is preferred to multiple one-time-only activities. This can rank as high as #2 in importance with some schools, and as low as #10. Use good judgment in considering what activities to mention—and which ones to support with articles. Gil Villanueva (Brandeis) says,

Newspaper clippings or Internet articles about unusual achievement/accomplishment or a student's volunteer involvement can be a plus. Any other piece of information that lends support to your application tends to be well received by admission officers, provided you do not overdo it.

Adds Don Bishop (Creighton), "These are worthwhile provided they are brief. It is interesting to read validations from independent sources. No more than one or two articles should be shared. Admissions committees have limited time to read applications."

Paul Marthers (Reed) points out, "Articles should only be included if they are unusual or outstanding. Clips of articles written for newspapers are acceptable, but no more than three should be included."

Eric Simonelli (University of Rhode Island) states,

At URI, we evaluate students holistically and encourage all students to get involved in their high school and in their local community. The more a student has experienced outside the classroom, the better we get to know a student. This information can sometimes be effectively shared through newspaper articles.

Personalized Cover Letter

Opinion on whether to include a personalized cover letter with your application ranges from "very useful" and "great idea" to "not necessary" and "don't bother." Where it can be appropriate and useful are the following scenarios:

Paul Marthers (Reed) states: "A personalized cover letter probably won't matter, *unless the letter cites an encounter or interview with me.*"

Adds Don Bishop (Creighton): "Generally, a personalized cover letter is not needed; most applications, through the essay topics or personal statement options, give students a chance to state why they are interested in the college. If no such outlets are made available, a brief, one-page cover letter stating the student's specific interest in the college is useful and appropriate."

Gil Villanueva (Brandeis) says, "While not necessary, a personalized cover letter is particularly effective in highlighting something specific about your application or in expressing a significant interest."

Geographic Region Represented/Ethnic Backgrounds/First in Family to Go to College

Special circumstances rank from #4 to #10 to not at all important, depending on the institution. As some admissions deans point out, if the school already has students enrolled representing 47 or 48 of the United States and you happen to live in one of the few states not enrolled, you might get a second glance. But this would be after all other criteria have been considered.

Chris Muñoz, Vice President for Enrollment, Rice University, states that the university tries to accept bright and promising students from a range of socioeconomic, cultural, geographic, and other backgrounds. He notes:

We consider an applicant's race or ethnicity as a factor in the admission process and believe that racial and ethnic diversity is an important element of overall educational diversity. Though race or ethnicity is never the defining factor in an application or admissions decision, we do seek to enroll students from underrepresented groups in sufficient and meaningful numbers as to prevent their isolation and allow their diverse voices to be heard. We also seek students whose parents did not attend college, as well as students from families with a well-established history of college-level education. Rice places a premium on recruitment of students, regardless of their races or ethnicities, who have distinguished themselves through initiatives that build bridges between different cultural, racial, and ethnic groups. In so doing, we endeavor to craft a residential community that fosters creative, intercultural interactions among students, a place where prejudices of all sorts are confronted squarely and dispelled.

Extraordinary Skill or Ability (Musical, Artistic, Athletic)

The importance of a special skill or ability is totally in the eye of the beholder, ranking from #2 to #10 in importance. If a student does possess a unique talent or skill in one of these areas, it can be a big plus if it brings something to a college that is lacking. The classic example is with the French horn or oboe player with eight years of training applying to a school with an orchestra or marching band missing that instrument: This can be of significant importance, provided all academic criteria is within an acceptable median range for the school.

Additional Factors

Following are a few additional factors that admissions professionals consider when deciding whether to admit a student.

Relative Rankings

Don Bishop (Creighton) noted four additional characteristics that are essential in weighing the quality of the student's competition at their respective high school. These include the following:

- ACT/SAT median for senior class
- Percentage of seniors taking the ACT/SAT

- Percentage of seniors that are National Merit Scholars or Commended

- Percentage of seniors attending four-year colleges

"A student ranking in the top 10 percent at one school may be judged to have comparable rank to a student ranked in the top 20 percent at another school if it is determined that the student at the second school had twice as many students at their school of high caliber as did the student at the other school," he advised.

Personal Qualities

Gil Villanueva (Brandeis) stated that following the most important criteria of transcript, rank in senior class, GPA, and strength of academic curriculum, personal qualities join the letters of recommendation as the #2 criteria (the application essay is ranked #3 at Brandeis). He stated, "The Committee on Admissions at Brandeis University carefully accounts for an institutional fit; i.e., we ask ourselves if the applicant possesses the kind of persona we find to be a match with our community."

Of course, not every school will necessarily require all of these components. And as was evident in the expert recommendations offered by admissions deans from around the country in chapters 2 and 3, schools consider the value of these items according to widely differing scales.

Key Points: Chapter 6

- Depending on the institution, the most critical parts of the admission application are your high school transcript, academic progress report, standardized test scores, strength of academic curriculum, class rank, GPA, application essay, and letters of recommendation.

- Other items that might be requested or that you might be allowed to include for consideration are parent/peer evaluations, work samples/portfolio, student resume, personal statement, student interview, extracurricular activities, volunteerism/community service, special circumstances, and extraordinary skill or ability.

- Admissions offices may also consider additional factors such as relative rankings and personal qualities.

Chapter 7

Actual Winning Essays to Inspire You

This chapter features actual essays used to support successful admission to the school that the student ultimately attended. The idea behind presenting actual essays is trifold:

- To dispel the idea that you must be a writer of the caliber of Ernest Hemingway or Marcel Proust and capable of earning a Pulitzer in order to write a compelling college-application essay. These are real, unedited essays written by real high school seniors with widely varied backgrounds, accomplishments, and areas of interests. Virtually all of these essays worked: They secured acceptance into one or more colleges, including the schools that these students are all now attending.

- To inspire and motivate you to think, "Gee, that's an interesting story! It makes me want to know more about this student"—and then reflect, "Wow! I have interesting stories about me that I could talk about—details to share that might make someone want to know more about *me*." Obviously, sample essays sourced on the Internet, in this book, or from any other book are not presented for the purposes of being copied. You are a completely unique individual. Your essay must be authentic and totally *you*.

- To demonstrate many different roadmaps you can use to tell your own special story.

Many of these same students willingly provided their best advice, based on personal experience. Some of this wisdom is reflected throughout this chapter; other strategies appear in chapter 5. The titles for each of these essays were *not* supplied by any of the students; they represent my best effort to briefly describe and categorize the themes of the essays.

> **Note:** *These essays are published exactly as they were submitted. As author, I did not take any editorial license; and, in fact, I resisted the urge to do a little additional polishing. Bottom line: These essays are authentic and have otherwise not been "wordsmithed" or professionally edited in any way.*

Many students shared with me the sentiment that if they were writing their essays now (whether they are freshmen in college or about to graduate with their baccalaureate degrees), the content would look very different. They also said that in just looking back at what they had written a year or several years ago, they would make lots of revisions today. However, this is reflective of their continued college-level learning (and the fact that all writers know: You can *always* go back to your work and refine, revise, and polish it).

Each essay includes the student's actual first name and the first initial of their last name, along with the name of the college or university for which the essay was successfully used and that the student is now attending. Where identifying details—school name, hometown, and the like—are mentioned, these have been altered slightly to ensure student privacy.

The essays that follow are grouped into categories that partially reflect one of the themes represented in the content. Some essays speak to multiple themes, and you'll see how these students accomplish that approach.

Essay Theme #1: Why This School?

Why Duke?

In Camila's own words: "I felt that I had done some of my best writing my junior year of high school in my AP English class. As a result I used several of my essays that I had written for the class and then modified them to fit college prompts. Look over your essays as much as possible. Read them out loud, proofread them, and have another person proofread them. Leave them alone before you submit them officially and then come back to make sure they are flawless. Lastly, take risks on your essays. Try to break away from the standard mold and write something that will really show who you are. You want your quirks and personality to come through in your writing; you want to make an impression."

This is the first of three essays written by Camila G., all for Duke University. The other two appear under the categories of "Music, Literature, and Performing Arts" and "Making a Difference."

If you are applying to Trinity College of Arts and Sciences, please discuss why you consider Duke a good match for you. Is there something in particular at Duke that attracts you?

In a "letter to myself" from my late elementary school years, I expressed fervent sentiments about Duke University. I knew little about Duke's clubs, courses or curriculum; my interests lay in the realm of Coach K. As a little girl in Husky country, there were few who approved of my affection for Corey Maggette, Shane Battier and the Cameron Crazies. I did not mind. My allegiance was to the Blue Devils. I am now a high school senior whose predilection for Duke transcends the commercial esteem of my fourth and fifth grade self. Now, not only do I admire the intangible spirit, pride and character of the university, but also I am drawn to the boundless academic, social and extracurricular opportunities that Duke has to offer. Having aspirations to one day become a judge, I am certain that many of these opportunities, classes such as social inequality, theories of social justice and American political system, would make Duke an exceptional match for me.

Outside of the classroom, Duke's Latino Life Connection program is particularly appealing to me. In my own town, I have observed that the clique comprised of most of my Hispanic peers is noticeably confined (by choice) to one area of the lunch room, is evidently congregated in the hallways during classes and is conspicuously absent from any of my honors and advanced placement courses. The students in this group are categorized by themselves and others as "ghetto." Though I am often angered that this clique helps to perpetuate negative stereotypes about Latinos, I believe there are ways to promote better images for Hispanics. Adolescents, especially those who consistently see their ethnicity represented by "thugs", "pimps" and "homies", need positive, relatable role models. Latino Life Connections is a means toward establishing these affirmative connections with children and families. Additionally, "Turning the Page" combats hindrances in reading and writing comprehension that affect the achievement gap.

As a student at Duke, I cannot promise that I will win adoration across a maddened nation in March. However, I can promise that I will wholeheartedly involve myself every day to influence my peers, my professors and the people around me.

—Camila G., Duke University

Why Tufts?

In Nick's own words: "The number-one piece of advice I would give is *be yourself.* Don't try to think too much about what you are writing and whether or not you 'sound smart.' Admissions counselors have tons of essays to read, and one that is truly written in your voice (meaning they can get an idea of what kind of person you are from your language) would be much more interesting and attention-getting than something you wrote trying to sound scholarly."

This is the first of two essays written by Nicholas M., both for Tufts University. The other essay appears under the category of "Challenges, Accomplishments, and New Adventures."

"Education does not accomplish anything if it does not stretch your mind, if it does not force you to think about things in different ways, if it does not challenge you to examine some of your assumptions," writes Provost Jamshed Bharucha in Tufts' admissions viewbook. Describe the aspect of Tufts' curriculum or undergraduate program that prompted your application to the university's Class of 2010.

Perhaps the one thing I found most attractive about Tufts when I visited this past spring was that it offers a nice blend of rigorous engineering education with rich variety in the humanities. I can be comfortable knowing that I can focus on a major for a career, and still have wide options of taking other classes in things that interest me just to satisfy my curiosity. For example, Tufts was the first school I visited where you can minor in something called "Musical Instrument Engineering." I heard one of the student tour guides talk about this during my visit, and I found it pretty unusual, but fascinating at the same time.

I was also pleased to find out that Tufts offers opportunities for students to do research both inside and outside of class. Working out engineering solutions to real-world problems seems like one of the best ways to get students ready for real-world jobs once they graduate. I have always loved making things and pondering how things work, and I believe I would feel right at home studying engineering at Tufts University.

—Nicholas M., Tufts University

Finding a School That's an Ideal Match

In Russell's own words: "Keep your target audience in mind as you write, try to emphasize qualities that would be appealing to people on admission boards, things that make you different than other applicants. Often students have some say in the acceptance of an applicant, so don't be too dry. If you pretend to be someone you are not, you have a big risk of ending up in a place you don't belong. Give yourself enough time, but if you do it too soon you'll risk having an essay that doesn't accurately represent you as a person."

When I began planning for college, I looked for a very rigorous school focused on math and science. I want a school that will be extremely challenging academically. After four years, I want to look back and be able to say that I learned as much as possible. Using these criteria, Caltech quickly rose to the top of my list. The academic program seems to be very vigorous and varied. The housing system is also very appealing to me. To a New Englander who is getting sick of cold winters, the Southern Californian weather doesn't look too bad either.

© JIST Works

Most importantly however, the atmosphere of the school seems to be exactly what I want. I long to be in a place where I am surrounded by people at least as motivated as I am, and where everyone has diverse interests. I want a place where I can do meaningful research, even as an undergraduate. Above all else, I want to be in an environment where I know I can trust everyone around me. The Honor Code of Caltech addresses this concern very well. On many levels, it seems that Caltech perfectly matches what I desire in a college.

I also think that I am exactly what Caltech is looking for in a student. I have always done well in school, but I have never felt like the curriculum was pushing me to my limits. I spend a lot of my free time learning about things I am interested in, and I have acquired a lot of knowledge about a wide range of topics, from Japanese to music theory to electronics. I am always hungry for more information.

I believe I would contribute greatly to the college community. I try to be the best person I can, and I am always trying to improve myself. I work well under pressure, and I try not to let the pressure affect my attitude. I try to keep one step ahead of stress by maintaining an optimistic disposition and keeping things in perspective.

I have a wide range of non-academic interests that bring me a lot of pleasure. I am a big fan of music from the eighties, and I have an embarrassingly large collection of Synth-Pop albums on vinyl. I enjoy watching campy movies, especially seventies and eighties horror movies. I have always enjoyed computer games, although these days it seems I spend more time programming than playing them. I also occupy my time with solving Rubik's cubes, juggling, and yo-yoing. I think my sense of humor and fun will be a benefit to the community.

Of all the colleges I have investigated, Caltech seems to be the closest to my ideal. I think that I could contribute much to the community, and I think that the community and the academics would do much to improve me as a scholar and as a person.

—Russell M., California Institute of Technology

Essay Theme #2: Influential Person

Two Modern-Day Heroes—to Me

In Billy's own words: "Do not stress about college applications; start them early if you can—and you will not need to worry. Write about something you are interested in and it will come easy and fast. Then you can take your time to fine-tune it."

The next two essays were written by Billy R., both for Colby College.

A Second Dad: My Football Coach

Tom Parr is a man who has greatly influenced my life. In his prime, Tom was one of the best quarterbacks in Colgate University history. Dazzling teams with his incredible footwork and speed, Tom was so impressive running the ball that he was selected for the Division I All-East team; that squad included Tony Dorsett, winner of the Heisman Trophy and future member of the Dallas Cowboys. Tom Parr may have had a similar athletic future, but he badly injured his knee and was no longer able to play football.

However, Tom is still active in the game as the head coach of the Hopkins football team. I have admired Coach Parr since seventh grade and could not wait to play under his guidance. Now, as captain and quarterback of the Hopkins team, my relationship with Coach Parr is as strong as can be between a coach and player. As captain, I have met with him numerous times to discuss the team; he expects leadership and dedication from me during the season and throughout the year. As quarterback, the position at which he excelled, I listened to every word he said to help me become a better player.

As best friend of his son, Dana, I have visited the Parr home on many occasions. Coach Parr's hospitality has been more than I could ask for, making me feel part of the family. When not in classes at school, I am usually in his office. In fact, this is the first place my parents call when they need to talk to me!

Coach Parr has helped me grow from the boy who arrived the first day of preseason freshman year to the man who left the field after my last game senior year. Coach Parr knows that some players can be yelled at without being bothered by it, while other players will take it personally. As the quarterback and a leader of the team, I have been yelled at plenty (third, I think, only to his two sons, Dana and Andrew). At the end of the season he thanked me for not complaining about him yelling at me all year. However, through his passion he was able to convey to me the importance of personal commitment to improvement. By pushing me beyond my limits, he has helped me become a man on and off the field.

After our final game this year, I thanked him for all he had done for me. Tears filled my eyes as I stood on the field with my arms around the man who had become a second father to me. In turn, I knew I had made Coach Parr proud when I looked into his eyes as he handed me the "For Love of the Game" award from my teammates. His guidance and instruction, now part of me, will serve me well throughout my life. It has been an honor to know Coach Parr as a coach and a man.

—Billy R., Colby College

© JIST Works

A Hero in My Dad

The motto of Wake Forest University is "Pro Humanitate". To me, these words describe a philosophy in which people are eager to help and serve others. Such people think not of themselves first, but rather of others, even at the risk of their own lives for others. Hero is a word thrown around all too lightly these days. A man is not a hero because he can run ninety yards for a touchdown, because he can slap a puck one hundred miles per hour into a goal, because he can make a basket from thirty feet.

I am lucky; I have been around real heroes my whole life. They are firefighters, brave men who risk death to save the lives and property of strangers. Courage is running into a burning building, while everyone else, even the rats, is running out.

My father is a firefighter who has risen through the ranks to become the Deputy Chief of the New Haven Fire Department. He loves his job (which, unfortunately, not many people can say about their careers) because he has been able to have fun at work with his colleagues, while having a direct, positive impact in the community. Unlike millionaire athletes who have been known to take days off due to sprained egos, my father has not missed one day of work, unless bedridden or injured, in his 32 years on the job.

In the firehouse, the firefighters casually joke and have a good time together; once the alarm bell rings, they become serious and focused, knowing that if one member of the team fails, lives can be lost. They have confidence that the man in front of them and the man behind them are professionals who not only will get the job done, but will protect them at all costs. That is why a special brotherhood exists among firefighters.

These brave men never boast about their accomplishments and the lives they have saved. After extinguishing a fire, they hold no self-aggrandizing press conferences. My father has been awarded numerous accolades for valor. I have never seen one of them except when I attended a ceremony in which he received a medal and several certificates; I have not seen them since. He feels that firefighting is simply his job, just like any other person's job.

It took the tragic events of September 11th for many people to realize that sports stars are not the real heroes. I have known this all along. I hope that in my lifetime I can possess half the bravery and courage that any firefighter displays every day.

—Billy R., Colby College

An Influential Uncle—a Valuable Lesson for Life

In Jamie's own words: "I found college essays to be difficult to write because of the topics. They can be pretty lame and at times insulting to my creativity. However, as impossible to answer as some of the questions may seem, everyone has something to say. Sometimes, it just takes longer to realize what your answer is. Therefore, I would suggest not forcing an answer just to get the essay written, but waiting until you have a moment where you realize what it is you want to say. The voice of your essay will sound more genuine and plus it won't be so painful to write. I guess the best advice I received was to write about something meaningful and not something that you think the admissions offices will like the best."

Family cookouts always meant laughter, corn on the cob and grass stains. My cousins' tiny yard had an above ground pool that kept six kids occupied for hours.

When the sun started to set, we'd nag the parents to join us. My uncle John was always the only one to oblige. He'd cannonball into the pool. Like leeches, we would cling to him, wanting to be thrown through the air or jump from his shoulders. One by one, he'd give us all turns flipping, jumping and splashing.

Last year on my cousin's 13th birthday, there was no cookout. Not that her family forgot. My uncle was in a hospital, strapped to a bed. For four years now, he has struggled with brain tumors, cancer, surgeries, hospital bills, medications, and scars. He struggles to stay awake long enough to eat breakfast and struggles with the hardships caused by his sickness. He can't drive anymore, he can barely hear, and he has lost most of the vision in his left eye. His face is badly deformed from surgery and he has to wear an eye patch. He can no longer throw anyone around the pool.

Helen Keller once said that one should "always look to the sun and you will never see the shadows." It is a philosophy that I have always been able to comprehend but am now able to live by because of my uncle.

There is no doubt that he is one of the bravest people I know. He faces each day with renewed enthusiasm, even though he knows he will have trouble just getting out of bed. When we get together, he is still the most animated person at the table, telling stories with gusto. His laughter still rings out no matter where we are.

For his everlasting optimism, I consider my uncle to be an influential figure in my life. I have always loved his personality and upbeat energy. However, until he was diagnosed, I didn't realize how truly admirable and valuable these traits were. His positive attitude and courage have taught *me* how to be a better person. He has taught me to look my challenges in the eye. He has taught me to cherish my day-to-day life, because simple things, like driving or sleeping, could vanish in a heartbeat.

© JIST Works

He also has set a high standard for compassion for others in spite of his own condition. When my Dad's family found out my grandmother was sick, he was among the first to visit, even though driving had become a hardship. This is one of the few times I have seen my father at a loss for words… actions like this have shown me the impact kindness can have. It has compelled me to be more considerate, even if it is small gestures like holding the door for someone, saying thank-you, or inviting someone new to sit at my lunch table.

The outlook on life that I have gained from my uncle is one that I would never have learned elsewhere. His courage in the face of such a terrifying situation has impacted me in more ways than he could ever know. He has shown me to look past petty stresses in life and to not let these anxieties impose upon my character. From my uncle's example, I have gained the motivation to always have a positive attitude and to spread that energy to everyone around me. On the volleyball court, I get my teammates excited to play, and this enthusiasm carries through in everything I do; it's contagious. Anyone who knows me will tell you that a prominent part of my personality is that positive energy.

My uncle has shown me the importance of optimism and how that positive approach to obstacles makes the road to success a smoother passage. I no longer fear that a bad quiz grade is the end of the world, or that a fight with my friend will be resolved. Rather than self-pitying, I look for solutions to my problems and find the motivation to make things better. Furthermore, I have learned that an encouraging disposition has the greatest impact on the people around you.

Helen Keller once also said that "optimism is the faith that leads to achievement. Nothing can be done without hope and confidence." I strongly believe that everything happens for a reason, and that my uncle's journey has been a part of my life as a lesson. He has taught me how to live by the meaning of this quote and how to make it my own. More importantly, I know how to pass this lesson on to other people, a truly priceless present to anyone.

—Jamie H., Dickinson College

An Influential Coach—On the Football Field (and Off)

In Marc's own words: "The best thing that I did for myself was taking a college writing course in my senior year in high school. It was offered during the first semester during the peak of college essay writing. The teacher structured the class primarily on writing college essays as well as other writing strategies. The teacher gathered a collection of previous college essay topics and also went into depth into the most common college essay themes that are typically used by college or university admissions offices. Throughout the semester I was able to write four well-critiqued essays that matched each of the typical admissions essay topics. It worked out that I was able to use one or more of each of the essays I had written for each college that I applied to. It was definitely well worth it and it helped strengthen my essays."

Character is created by the influences of other people in one's life. It takes an entire lifetime to build character. I have been exposed to many personalities in my short lifetime, but I believe the person who has had the most impact on my character is my football coach, Bob McNamara. His character and morals have become as much a part of me as any other person I know.

My coach has had an extraordinary influence on my life all throughout high school. He is more than just a coach; he is a mentor. Coach Mac is the kind of person that is not only there for his players on the football field but off the field as well. Going through my high school career with Coach has had a positive impact on my life. As I began to develop my own personality through my life at home and school, Coach was very supportive. He instilled in me values that will forever be a part of my life.

Coach always stressed commitment and that has helped me become the person that I am. The discipline and hard work that he teaches on the football field have transcribed into my everyday life. To become a good football player a person must put his heart into it. To excel at anything one must be committed. I have become a good football player and I have also achieved other goals because of my commitment. Through eight years of dedication to the Boy Scouts of America I earned my Eagle Scout Badge. Without a strong commitment to the program I could not have persevered in my pursuit. I also earned my confirmation because I attended every class with an eagerness to learn, and a devotion to my faith. Coach Mac taught me the importance of commitment and that has helped me achieve the goals that I have set in my life.

Because of coach's example I have also become a leader. I used to be the quiet player as a freshmen and sophomore, but as a senior I developed authority and charisma to become an effective captain of the football team. "Strive for perfection, but settle for excellence," is what coach always tells us, "but there is nothing wrong with being perfect either." Those words encourage me to strive to be the best player possible. As a result of my productivity on the football field other players look to me to be a role model. This role has made me a better person. Coach demonstrates that a leader needs to be a part of the team as well as a leader. I have used this in Boy Scouts as well. I was elected Senior Patrol Leader and was chosen to lead the entire troop. Coach Mac is the greatest leader I know and I have modeled his leadership and used on the field as well as other activities.

Coach Mac has done so much for me and his character became a part of mine as I continue to develop. He has also shown interest in helping me pursue a school that I can play football at as well as study what I intend to pursue. My life has been enriched with his bold character. Since Coach had been a positive influence

I am developing into a well-rounded individual. I have learned to tackle problems in life much like I tackle opposing players on the field because of Coach Mac. His pursuit for perfection, with morality and values a part of his quest, has become mine as well. I can only imagine where life can take me as I keep Coach a part of me.

—Marc G., Worcester Polytechnic Institute

A Grandfather's Influence by Example

In Meghan's own words: "Do not let the writing process edit your true character out of the essay. The essay should be of high quality, but do not let all the editing take the voice out of your work. The essay process seems overwhelming at first, but just think of something of importance to you and it will come naturally. My dad recommended to try using anecdotes in my essay. I feel that helped bring out my 'voice' a lot in comparison to 'I am special, choose me because.' This style allowed me to really own my essay and feel good about my work."

This is the first of two essays written by Meghan H., both for James Madison University. The other essay appears under the category of "Who Am I?"

In my seventeen years, many people have attempted to mold and shape my character. While I owe a tremendous amount of who I am to my parents, teachers, and peers, I sometimes find others have had just as significant an influence on me by the way they present themselves. By observing those people, I have been able to absorb vital characteristics that I use and will continue to use my whole life. One person who has taught me is my grandfather. My grandfather has instilled in me invaluable lessons through his wisdom, humor, and work ethic.

While walking up the hills in the Bronx to the Court Deli, my grandfather often lags behind the crowd. For the past fifteen years our family has had season tickets to the Yankees, and it has become a custom to walk to the deli a few blocks up from the stadium. As I walk up the hill I slow down to keep my grandfather company. "Keep up with your dad, I am fine," he tells me. I take a few quick paces and catch up with my dad, but worry about my grandfather who follows a few steps behind. It is obvious that he is struggling to keep a steady pace, but the look of determination out weighs his pain. Every visit my dad suggests that we eat at the Stadium rather than go up to the diner, but my grandfather thinks of us and struggles up the hills every single Bronx visit.

Throughout his life, my grandfather has encountered many difficult obstacles and has conquered them all. As a cancer survivor, he has been tested mentally and

(continued)

(continued)

physically within the past few years. Throughout his sickness he has been careful because of his health, but never underestimates himself and pushes himself to his limit. I am an active participant in many clubs and sports during the school year, and I am often pushed to my limit. During a typical school day I have clubs, sports, and homework to accomplish while getting to bed at a reasonable hour. I prioritize, and schedule my time so I will not be overwhelmed. My parents still question my involvement in school activities, but rather than quitting I have chosen to conquer my obstacles, rather than falling apart. When I think of my grandfather's difficult experience with cancer, juggling extracurricular activities does not seem such an impossible task. To stretch myself is to be determined, and to be determined is to succeed. My grandfather has been determined throughout his life, having a successful business life while creating a loving family environment.

"Poppy, could you tell the story about California?" questions my younger cousin. All of the older members of the family, of which I am now included, sit back and smile at the favorite story that will once again be told. While most would avoid telling a self-effacing story, my grandfather just smiles and begins. "Remember that summer we were driving around California in that old rental car?" my grandfather begins.

"It had been a long day, the kids were cranky and I was just trying to get out of the parking lot." My dad starts laughing, "Yeah, but you couldn't get out the same way as everyone else." Anticipating the climax of the story we all begin laughing, but the younger children cannot comprehend what is so funny. "So I was trying to back out of a difficult spot, and my vision was blocked by all the kids sitting in the back seat. They chose not to mention that there was a big pole in the direct path of where I was backing up the car." My grandmother shakes her head and says, "We all saw it but we knew you would have bitten off our heads if we had said anything." My grandfather continues ignoring my grandmother's rebuttal.

"So, there I am in a hot rental car in a crowded parking lot after a long day and I ram directly into a pole."

My grandfather is not all about determination; he does have a funny bone even if it is self-effacing. After each meal the family does not get up but rather waits for him to start telling a story. Whether the story is about his experience in the Navy, road rage, or his children, there is always a punch line that tends to be aimed at himself. Some are not intended to be funny but his expressions and comments make it nearly impossible to maintain composure. I laugh along with the rest of my family, but I often find myself at school in a situation similar to those of my grandfather. I do not tell his jokes, but I find that I am often making jokes at my own expense. Every morning in the parking lot I pull in crooked in my parking space. It has become a ritual for me to back out of the spot and endure ridicule from witnesses. A few years ago I might not have been able to tolerate this, but I have accepted the fact that my inability to park is a weakness I cannot hide. My ability to laugh at myself stems from my grandfather's stories, but some stories were not meant to be funny, some were heartwarming while others showed determination.

My great-grandfather saved the local town newspaper from bankruptcy, and my grandfather did not think twice about taking over when his father was no longer able to work. My grandfather worked many years as the owner of the newspaper, a demanding job that required a lot of time and effort. Never quitting, my grandfather was with the newspaper through many difficult situations while raising a family. Although I do not yet have a family of my own, I have many responsibilities at school and in my town. Teaching Sunday school at my local church has been a Sunday tradition for the past four years. When I was asked to teach Sunday school, I was very excited to have the opportunity to work with children and thus dedicated myself to preparing lessons and working with the children. After a year, the Sunday school program had undergone changes, many fellow teachers were leaving and I had to decide whether to return in the fall. I chose to stay, wanting to give back to the church that I had grown up attending. I know through my grandfather's example of giving to his community despite setbacks, that quitting is not an option.

The ideals that my grandfather has instilled in me are not from lectures or copying notes. My grandfather influences me by example, not by telling me how to live my life. As I begin my venture through college next year, I will no longer have the comfort zone of my school district in which I have spent 13 years. I will be thrust into a new community into which I am prepared to integrate. As I do in high school, I will use the life skills that my grandfather taught me, and continue to establish myself wherever I go throughout life. Next year, I will not be able to rely on my grandfather's gentle push to encourage me. However, I know that through my actions his valuable lessons will always be with me.

—Meghan H., James Madison University

Essay Theme #3: Becoming a Teacher

Babysitter...to Mentor...to Teacher

In Jeff's own words: "The first thing to remember is to *not* stress. You have enough stress in your life and with everything going on, the worst thing you can do is stress yourself out more. Based on what the essay has to be about, brainstorm a bunch of different possibilities. The best way to write a good essay is to write about something that either interests you, or that you actually care about.

"Have a teacher (preferably an English teacher) read your essay to check for grammar and sentence structure. Nothing is worse than having errors on a paper that literally may decide whether or not you are accepted into a college. I wrote and revised my paper probably a total of 10 times. This allowed me to really make sure I had it exactly perfect and exactly the way I wanted it."

While I was watching the volleyball match, my cell phone ring pierced the air and broke the silence of the game. "Hello," I said. "Hey, Jeff, it's EJ. My parents never came to pick me up after my soccer game today, and I've been standing here for a half hour." "All right," I replied, "I'm leaving now and will be there in a few minutes." As I hung up the phone, I could tell from EJ's voice that he was upset. I jumped in the car and headed towards his school—glad that he could always count on me in an emergency, but more importantly I felt comfort knowing that he called me instead of standing alone in the dark.

Once I arrived at the school, I saw my little buddy as sad as could be, resting his head in his two hands. This was not the same boy who normally greets me by bouncing up and down with excitement. When he looked up and saw me approaching, his eyes lit up. As he moved towards my car, I saw the relief wash over his face because someone had finally come for him. "How are you, buddy?" I asked as he got into the car. "I'm fine; I just couldn't get a hold of my mom or dad so I called you," he said in an embarrassed tone. I could tell that he felt badly. "It's fine, EJ; don't worry about it. You know that if you ever need anything at all, you need only to pick up the phone, and I'll be there." As I peered over at the boy I've known for over a year, I realized how much EJ relies on me for emotional and moral support. When I first met him, EJ was just another kid I babysat, but after spending so much time with him, he has become more like a brother to me. He calls me after he's had a bad day, when he has a question, or anytime he just wants to talk. As we headed back to the game, I noticed EJ's anxiety waning and felt relieved myself knowing that he was comforted.

Working with children through babysitting, teaching summer school, and volunteering as a teacher's aid has taught me that treating kids fairly and respectfully creates a strong relationship. I've also learned that the key to teaching is showing children I care. Something as simple as complimenting their haircut gives them the attention they need from a male role model. This makes them feel safe, comfortable, and cared for, all of which are necessary for a relationship of truth and honesty. Working with children has truly had a dramatic effect on my life. I find it very gratifying, and I know that with commitment and perseverance I will reach my goal of becoming a teacher as well as a mentor because I believe, "All kids need is a little help, a little hope, and somebody who believes in them" [Earvin Johnson].

—Jeff F., Marist College

Planting the Seed to Become a Teacher

In Jason's own words: "If given a choice of topics, pick one that you can easily relate to. Don't try to impress them by writing about something you don't know about; it doesn't work. Write a rough draft without worrying about the number of words and have lots of people look over it. Ask parents, friends, and high school teachers. Rewrite it many times. High school

English teachers will help you with editing. Don't wait until the last minute. It takes time to get feedback from teachers. Try to have it done before your senior year."

In 500 words or less, tell us what your goals for the future are. What experiences have inspired those goals? What activities have you engaged in (or plan to) to reach those goals?

It's the first day of church school and I'm teaching the kindergarten class again this year. I'm excited; this year is going to be different because I'm the teacher and not a teacher's aid. The lesson I planned is the creation story. I explain to the children that God created everything. I then give the students paper and ask them to draw things created by God. One student draws a giant circle with a little circle in the corner. I ask him what it is and he tells me it's the Death Star. He explains that it was cool and God must have created it. I answer that God created everything even the Death Star. That's when I knew I wanted to be a teacher.

To prepare for becoming a teacher I decided to get involved in as many activities as possible that provide an opportunity to work with children. I have continued teaching church school for four years and have had countless experiences like the one above. I have worked at a Summer Camp as a Counselor in training and then as a counselor. I am currently working part-time at an after school program. It is a challenge to keep the children engaged in activities while maintaining discipline. One day it was particularly difficult because it was raining out and kids were stuck indoors. I decided to teach them a new game called toilet tag; similar to freeze tag except when you get frozen you make yourself a toilet seat and can't move until someone flushes you. Running and flushing, we played until their parents showed up. One kid left, in malcontent, asking if he could stay for another game. It's a good feeling knowing you made life more fun on a child's rainy day. I am also taking a child development class this year. In this class we learn how to take care of children and even have a preschool program. In the preschool program we learn how to plan lessons and deal with disciplinary issues, it is a great learning opportunity.

I love working with children because they are so eager to learn and it's fascinating to watch them grow and master new skills. This summer I was teaching my niece to ride a bike. She was so determined and just wouldn't give up no matter how many times she fell. After several hours, she finally mastered the skill. Her whole face lit up and she was so excited. I felt great knowing that I had helped her to feel so good about herself. I want to be a teacher so I can relive that feeling of helping children achieve their potential.

My goal for the future is to become an elementary school teacher and have a positive impact on many children. I'm hopeful that my background and what I expect to gain from my college experiences will allow me to achieve this goal.

—Jason C., Concordia University Chicago

Essay Theme #4: Athletics as a Backdrop

For Her, Running Is a Passion and a Lifestyle

In **Lindsey's own words:** "Write about something that you are passionate about because it will produce a much better essay. Never write one of the standard essay questions that the university provides for you because they are sick of reading those responses. Try to write about a topic of your own choice if that is an option to you. Write about something that shows you and displays good qualities about you to the school that you want to choose you over any other student."

Topic of Choice: What Is Passion?

Hanging above my bed is a Nike poster of a woman's legs completely covered in mud. The quotation on it reads, "My sport is your sport's punishment." Every time I look at the poster, I smile because the woman on the poster is a runner, and so am I. Running is not merely a sport to me, though, it is a passion. According to the dictionary, passion is a strong feeling of anger, love, or desire. According to me, passion is lacing up my sneakers and going on a long run in mud up to my knees, pouring rain, hail the size of golf balls, summer heat, or winter snow.

I did not look for the sport of running; it found its way into my life. Although I tried a variety of other sports and activities, they just never seemed to fit. I played soccer when I was growing up, but I realized that the aggressive nature was not quite in me when my coaches started yelling at me to stop saying "I'm sorry" when I stole the ball, and "Excuse me" when I bumped into someone. Running was not a compromise because nothing else was a perfect fit, however; running has taught me more about myself than anything else in my life.

Becoming a better runner has paralleled my becoming a better person. Running has not only taught me to work hard, but to love myself for my efforts. Because running is an individual activity, I have learned to enjoy my own company and to cherish the time to let my mind wander. Running is my way of releasing energy and relieving stress and pressures that I am feeling. In becoming a stronger person and a better runner, I have improved my confidence as well. Now as team captain, I take every opportunity to help younger runners and to instill in them some of my passion, so that they too will love the sport.

The mental capability that a person must have to be a devoted runner goes far beyond any knowledge gained from academics. This mentality must be developed through experience. Many people say that runners are crazy fanatics, and maybe I am. Regardless, I have learned that the will and drive to conquer my opponent

© JIST Works

and push forward against my body when it is telling me to stop is the most rewarding feeling I have ever felt. For me running is not just about racing or winning, it is a lifestyle that I choose to live. My long-term goal is to run a marathon and have fun doing it.

Louis Horst, who had a passion for dance, once said, "Dance for yourself. If someone else understands, good. If not, no matter. Go right on doing what interests you, and do it until it stops interesting you." I substitute "run" for dance in that quote, and think of it as the motivation to do what I love, never to give up my passion, and to keep running.

—Lindsey W., University of Connecticut

Perseverance and Determination

In Meg's own words: "Since I wrote about a unique, life-changing experience, I felt my essay was very sincere and truly me. Because I felt this way, I wasn't terribly upset when I got two rejection letters. It meant I couldn't find any excuses to say why I didn't get in. Therefore, I would say that after going through a list of possibilities to pick from, choose a topic that actually means something to you and can result in a heartfelt essay.

"However, I have to say this was my common application essay (which all my schools took). For Carleton, I had to write six different any-length responses. Don't get too hung up on those because I feel those shouldn't take days to complete. I also think essays should be short, sweet, and to-the-point—unless your personality is to write 10-paragraph essays for every response. If that's the case, then go right ahead. But, in conclusion, don't make up a fake personality for a college to like you more since it's you who'll be going there."

When I was fourteen, I biked 3,700 miles in nine weeks across North America from Sharon, Vermont to Seattle, Washington. Each day brought new experiences that will stay with me forever more. This trip taught me to make choices for good reasons and hope the choices I make will help others.

Day 15. 66 miles into Wardsville, Ontario, Canada. Warning of "a slight chance of rain."

I reached the intersection of Rt. 2 and Rt. 16 by myself, startled to find midnight black clouds looming in the sky. I slowed down to hop off my bike and stare at the clouds. However, my teenage silliness distracted me when I spotted a speed limit sign noting "Maximum: 90". I took a picture of the sign measuring kilometers rather than a picture of Mother Nature's darkest pallet I've ever seen.

(continued)

(continued)

My trek into unknown weather conditions continued on as I kicked up my kick-stand and pushed down my right pedal. Despite how bad the weather seemed, I was in an optimistic mood, and soon I started cheerfully singing to myself. My singing seemed to have a positive impact upon my physical state of cycling that day.

Every minute that passed, the wind worsened - getting stronger and becoming more of a headwind. Every minute that passed, I examined my surroundings more: the different kinds of trees standing proudly, the grass swaying, the occasional rabbit scurrying into a hole, cars passing me cautiously. Every minute that passed, I felt more linked with the world.

As the rain came, my smile grew. As the rain turned to hail, I sang louder until I was nearly shouting. I was biking into the clouds of death, and I was certainly NOT going to have a miserable time doing it.

When the hail began to bite at my skin, I realized it was time to put on my rain gear. Once I stopped, the wind shoved my bike to the ground. The wind also took to bullying the tall grass: it was now flattened against the ground. *Maybe it's time to find shelter.* Normally trees would do the job, but the last one I had seen was a few miles back. I lifted my head up to start looking for houses.

I soon picked out a house only a half a mile up the road; walking my bike up the driveway, I rehearsed my plea for shelter until the storm passed. When I squinted through the rain, I saw a shirtless man, dog at his heels, ushering me into his garage. I graciously thanked him and walked out of the rain. We made small talk, mostly concerning my biking trip. In an hour I was back on my bike, joined by three others from my group, watching the light gray sky fading into pale blue.

That day was just one of the times I felt how connected the world is. The weather, the flora and fauna, the people - life in general. What one thing does matters to others, whether good or bad, fulfilling a purpose or just randomly, but nonetheless - every action has a reaction.

I found my new outlook on life while laughing and singing into that overpowering wind. I will be happy in what I do. I'll laugh at obstacles that try to stop me. I'll smile at the world because that's how it should be treated.

—Meg A., Knox College

Going the Distance: On the Course…and in School

In Jayson's own words: "I would create an outline of what material you would like to include in your entry essay. Next, I would produce multiple rough drafts until the final piece that is desired is accomplished. Also, I would have multiple people (three to four) read through your essay and critique it because chances are, multiple people will read your essay. This helps pick out certain mistakes others may miss and enriches your work."

State your favorite quote and explain its importance to you.

"To give anything less than your best is to sacrifice the gift." –Steve Prefontaine

This quotation speaks to me on a number of different levels. It affects my approach towards everyday life, athletic endeavors, and most importantly, education.

For those of you who may not know, Steve Prefontaine was arguably the best distance runner in the world throughout the late 1960s and into the 1970s. Many had claimed he would win the next summer Olympics in 1976 had he not passed away in a traffic accident in 1975. I model my running habit after Prefontaine's saying (mentioned above). Whether I am not into a race mentally or the pain is just too unbearable, I work through these roadblocks continuously to the finish line. I finish the race hard and strong, despite these weaknesses that are trying to hold me down. I realize that it is only a race and I do not want to be bogged down with the thought of "what if" the rest of the day.

A tradition highly valued at Biddeford High School is student participation in extracurricular activities. I take great pride in the organizations I am involved with at school. Participating in multiple clubs can be a challenging and time consuming task, but if balanced correctly, it can truly better a person both mentally and physically. I learned how to manage my time and prioritize the events in my life, as well as develop my approach to communicating with peers.

Growing up within a school system that encourages strong academic excellence, I developed a desire to want that seemingly unattainable level of success. Throughout my entire high school career, I have been enrolled in accelerated courses with the same core group of fifteen students. Placement into such an environment entices students to become highly competitive with one another in hopes of achieving their personal best. It is in situations like these where I learned very quickly that I must work harder than all my peers if I wished to stand out in the end.

This quote best exemplifies my feelings and beliefs toward obtaining an exceptional education. It expresses in words the actions I take on a daily basis in reaching my scholastic goals. I feel you are born with the inner ambition to strive and do your best, no matter what obstacles may lay in your path. It is up to the beholder how they with to exert these powers. Fortunately, I believe I am of a rare breed of students today who enjoy learning and broadening their education. I am willing to read that extra book, stay after school for help, or choose a study session over a sporting event if it means I will understand the topic in discussion. Through the views of my teachers I have come to see that it is better to get ahead when you can than stay back as just another member of the pack.

—Jayson N., University of Maine–Orono

Kathy, Softball, and Bugs

In Caitlin's own words: "I think it's important to write something that shows who you are, not necessarily who 'they' want you to be. When you're writing, try not to think about what the person reading your essay will be thinking; just think about whether this accurately depicts you and your personality. Even if it's a really dry and boring question, try to insert pieces of your personality, though I don't think chummy humor is the greatest idea. By looking at the question from an unusual viewpoint or adding personal experiences or ideas, the attention of the reader may be more easily maintained.

"Another thing is that even though it's nice to have people to read your essay for you, I think it sometimes encourages you to change your own unique voice. I know when writing my essay, I was very encouraged to change the last line. Luckily, I decided not to. It was this line that stuck out to a reader and clinched me as a recipient of a $700 scholarship from a local organization. Although other people's advice is often helpful, sometimes a person has to stick to his guns and write what he thinks does the best job of answering the question and depicting personality.

"Lastly, I found that the best strategy for writing these sometimes painful essays is sitting down, writing out everything that your brain thinks of in a very rough draft, taking a small break, and coming back to review. I just sort of made a really fast rough draft just to get all my ideas down, and then spent more time editing and changing what needed fixing. This way, you get a base essay done quickly, and then you put most of your efforts into improving what you have, rather than writing your essay slowly and agonizing over sentence structure and word choice. All that can be worried about later. In my experience, this was the best way to attack writing an application essay."

In my wise old age of seventeen, I have finally come to the conclusion that high school is not so much about what classes I take or what terrible grade I get on my calculus test, it's about appreciating the whole experience of being a high school student. I have decided that high school is about the things I *take away* from my time spent inside these blue walls. I have met some of my best friends here and have had some excellent fun under the noses of the librarians. I have become divulged in the game of softball, which has allowed me to develop a real sense of responsibility and school spirit. Through this school, I have branched out into community service at the local community center. Lyman has also supplied me with the preparation I need to move on to college, and convinced me of what I would like to do in college and after.

© JIST Works

When I'm on the softball diamond, I'm no longer Kate, I am now Kathy. For one reason or another, my teammates have adopted this nickname for me. In practice I am either Kathy, Kath or sometimes, Mom. I'm not sure how I adopted these names, but I can't say I don't enjoy it. As a freshman, I didn't realize that softball would have such a significant effect on me as it has proved to have. Not only has my name changed, my whole demeanor has changed. As a freshman I was force-fed into being the starting catcher because there was no one else on the team who could catch. Since then, I have become a team captain and a member of the All-Conference team. Softball has taught me about being responsible and reliable. Because I am a captain, I have to set an example for the younger girls. So when we go slogging up a hill for conditioning, I can't complain, I just have to do it. When the equipment is not put away, I don't order a tiny freshman to do it, I just do what needs to be done. It's important to me to mature and responsible so as to pull the whole team up with me. Softball has also built my confidence and self-esteem while introducing me to a whole new set of friends; my teammates. There are a lot of girls on the team that I never see in school, but when we're on the field, we are united for the same goal and we are all cemented together as team-mates and friends. Being a part of this team gives me something to work hard for and use my competitiveness to achieve a goal. Having that medal placed around my neck after winning the Class S State Championship was a culmination of all that hard work that my teammates and I had put in. Representing Lyman on the softball field has proved to be an opportunity that has changed me in so many positive ways.

Upon entering high school, I also began spending more and more time at the local community center where I learned many things I could not learn in school. One of my first experiences at the center was chaperoning an all-girl slumber party for third and fourth graders. Since I don't have any younger siblings, the thought of spending the whole night with fifty screeching little girls was quite daunting. But I did it, and only suffered a lack of sleep and some minor damage to my eardrums. Since that night, I have become a youth representative to the Wilmington Youth and Family Services Board of Directors. I am also in the process of setting up a Youth Advisory Board with another youth board member to involve the younger local teenagers. Volunteering as well as working at the center has introduced me to the happenings of my small yet complex community. Also, I have spent more time with kids in the past two years as I have in my whole life. As screechy as their little voices are, I have learned that I really do enjoy the company of the little ones. By being so closely involved with the central point of my community, I have learned a lot about the needs of my town. But most importantly, my experiences at the center have shown me that I cannot disregard the society around me. I like being a part of a body that changes my town for the better. I have found that involvement in community outside the walls of Lyman allows me to be connected to my local society and the inhabitants of my town.

(continued)

(continued)

As I head off to college, the ever looming question is brought to the foreground: "So what do you want to do after college?" The common inquisition of relatives, I am finally able to answer this question. In the fall I will be attending Rensselaer Polytechnic Institute where I will be majoring in biology. Deciding to be a biology major was not a hard decision for me. Once reaching high school I came to realize that science is definitely what interests me the most. However, I didn't exactly know where I wanted to go with that until I took AP biology. I quickly discovered that environmental and natural biology is what takes my fancy. By also taking biodiversity I have learned that in the field is where I belong. I therefore would like to achieve my degree in biology with a focus in environmental biology and then hopefully be able to work in field research. Who knows what may happen though, I could change my mind and major in fashion and design. Nah, I kind of doubt it. I don't think my professors would approve of my bug collection.

—Caitlin S., Rensselaer Polytechnic Institute

A Running Pursuit…and Not Giving Up

In Brian's own words: "My only advice would be to not be afraid to research the school in greater detail to tailor your essay to the school's attitude or ideals. The best advice I received was just to write about something that either affected me greatly or that I could honestly relate to, which I received from my parents and my English teacher."

"Now if you are going to win any battle you have to do one thing. You have to make the mind run the body. Never let the body tell the mind what to do. The body will always give up. It is always tired morning, noon, and night. But the body is never tired if the mind is not tired. When you were younger the mind could make you dance all night, and the body was never tired…. You've always got to make the mind take over and keep going."

—George S. Patton

This quote is by General George Patton who was not only an army general, but also a 1912 Olympian. What Patton is saying here is that when the mind takes control of the body anything is possible. Several years ago upon entering high school, I took up running. Since then, I would say that this quotation reflects my personal philosophy not only in running, but also in life. My mind runs my body on the track and off morning, noon, and night. Running was not always something I enjoyed; it was just a sport I had chosen to do my first year in high school. On the track that year, I knew I not only had the physical talent, but that I had a mind that loved to drive through pain and exhaustion to achieve a difficult goal.

© JIST Works

However, it was not so easy for me to use Patton's advice this year in my final cross country season. I started the season as the number one runner for my team, and I fell in status as the season went on. I was injured after my first race and forced into a three-week period of time off from exercise. Now after an entire summer of training, I found myself completely out of shape as a result of this time off. When I was finally ready to begin training again, I came down with an ear infection and a cold and could not regain my status as the number one runner. It was difficult to lose this status in a sport I am not only good at but that I love; however, I was happy enough to be helping my team and to still be running at all.

According to Patton's concept of mind over body, I remained, strong but still had no legs underneath me to carry out a completely successful season. The season was not a complete failure, however, because it helped me get into shape a little more for the next season of indoor track. This particular season also showed me another side to Patton's philosophy. I did everything I could not to give up, and in that sense, I let my mind tell my body it could not hold me to a bad season whether I was in peak condition or not in each race. This evolved my philosophy. Although my body was limited despite my mind's power to say otherwise, I did not let my body's limitations allow me to give up. It is this philosophy—an endless desire in the mind to achieve a goal no matter what obstacles you come across—and Patton's ideal that I refer to now and always will.

—Brian W., Dickinson College

As a Flexible Gymnast, Her Ability to Adapt Is Tested by Hurricane Katrina

In Shelley's own words: "Write about something you know really well. In doing so you ensure that the essay you end up with is something that speaks of something very personal to you. It also helps the quality of the essay itself in that you care about what you're writing. If you write about a topic that isn't close to you or even that significant, you could end up with an essay that isn't very personal or as meaningful as an essay written about something important. It's also a good idea to write about a conflict you had or a trial you had to go through that had significant meaning to you and you feel demonstrates your qualities."

A Change of Plans

Shelley graduated from high school in June 2005. She knew well before that time that she'd been accepted at Tulane University, where she hoped to study civil engineering. She had done the following for her Tulane application:

"I was asked to complete an extra project to apply for additional scholarships that they felt I was eligible for. I was sent a piece of 8.5" × 11" paper with a small 2" × 2" box in the middle, and using that I was asked to create something that represented me. What I did was make a puzzle with myself in the box in the center and all of the things I'm involved in or interested in around the outside."

The result? Her project earned her the Presidential Scholarship ($22,000 for each year of her undergraduate studies).

Unfortunately, Shelley had to give up that generous scholarship when the college of her dreams was nearly swept away in the tidal surge and catastrophic flooding by Hurricane Katrina on August 28 and 29, 2005 (right after new undergraduates had moved into their residence halls to begin their college careers). By the first week in September, Tulane and other universities in the Greater New Orleans area that was devastated by the storm announced that the fall semester was officially cancelled. Shelley had to scurry quickly—but with her fine academic record and other accomplishments, the University of Connecticut welcomed her into the College of Engineering as part of the class of 2009.

Balance beam is the event that makes or breaks a gymnast. A four-inch wide beam of minimally padded metal leaves no room for error. A slight balance check, a minute slip to one side, and off the beam you go. It can take months, if not years, to be comfortable with a skill. But the back handspring was no new skill for me. I had performed it in competitions and done it hundreds of times in practice with confidence and precision. It was as if my brain had been on automatic up to that moment. I never thought twice about what I was doing; I just did it. I would mount the beam and stand one foot in front of the other feeling the sandy texture of the leather and my toes as they gripped the four inch wide beam. I would swing my arms, bend my knees, pitch myself over backwards, then launch off my hands and land back on my feet. But there I was palms sweaty, mouth dry, head spinning. I felt like I was standing at the edge of a precipice and had to dive backwards off of it. At the end of months of hard work, I couldn't move.

That was three years ago, and I still stand on the beam and feel the same fear race through me. The only difference now is that I do it anyway. I get up on the beam and go because I refuse to let my fear end my career. After ten years of late night practices, rigorous summer schedules, challenging competitions, and the sheer physical trial of it all, fear is not going to drive me from the sport I love.

© JIST Works

There have been so many opportunities to quit along this rough road to conquering my fear. My coach has told me that I don't have to even work beam if it's too hard to get over my fear. Even my parents have said that if I'm having a hard time with the back handspring, I can drop the sport. The idea of giving up beam or leaving the sport is not an acceptable alternative. I would forever plague myself with thoughts of "What if I did this?" or "What if I tried harder?" And I would always feel disgusted with myself for not having fought through my fear. So, I haven't given up. I have not let myself be defeated. Fear, if anything else, makes you aware of your capabilities, provides a chance to grow and improve, and creates an opportunity to overcome challenges. This is my last year as a high school gymnast, so the pressure and drive to overcome my fear is even greater. "Pressure is a privilege," Billie Jean King once said, "Champions adjust." I may not win the State meet or even make the National competition, but champions aren't only the ones who win. They're the ones who work the hardest for their goals.

—Shelley P., Tulane University and University of Connecticut

Shattering a Track Record—and Feeling the Adrenaline

In David's own words: "Do everything you can to find someone who knows what they're doing. We worked on college essays in my AP English class. We did a lot of peer review, sure, but when it really came down to it, the most important advice came from her *[David's AP English teacher]*. I would say that college juniors and seniors should actively seek out someone who is knowledgeable about the college admissions process and can spend at least two to three sessions with them, discussing the topic first, then a first draft, then a second draft, etc.

"Keep your sentences short—you're not going to be able to explain your life story in a one- to two-page essay if you use flowery language and extended descriptions. It's okay to use imagery and all of that, just don't go overboard and start writing Faulkner-esque sentences that go on for a paragraph. Secondly, I'd say work out your vocabulary. The other thing is to avoid constructions like 'It is obvious that,' or 'It is clear that.' These are completely unnecessary—to what does the 'it' refer? Likewise, the construction 'there are' just screams eighth grade—again, to what does the 'there' refer? It's just fluff, and fluff is the last thing you want in a college essay. You're trying to encapsulate a wide range of things here—your personal style, whatever you're talking about, your ability to write, and probably more things I can't think of right now. Why put in fluff when you have so much to do?"

People have told me that I look as if I'm going to kill someone before I start a race. This is partially true; by pacing about and focusing my thoughts, I put myself in the right competitive state of mind before I run. The more important the meet, the more intense my routine becomes, and never was this so evident as when Midland's 400-meter relay team was competing at the State Open Championships. After I finished stretching prior to my race, I paced and sprinted periodically to keep my legs warmed up. I marched purposefully around the infield for nearly 30 minutes that day, throwing the baton from hand to hand in rhythm to the steps I took. Never had I felt more alive than before that race. We four runners had worked from the beginning of the season to surpass every school record set by previous teams and to show every large school in Texas that four suburbanites from a school of 500 could compete with the finest athletes in the state. We had reached a level that no one from our school ever had, and as I walked toward the starting line with my team, I thought to myself: "Here we are, in the fastest heat with the lowest seed and nothing to lose."

As my team and I waited for the previous heats to conclude, I was momentarily gripped by the agonizing fear of being "the weakest link." My mind was over-whelmed by "what-ifs," but quickly I was able to reassure myself. As the officials sorted out the heats, I thought back to the sweltering Sunday afternoons when I had gone to the track for "300's," our most difficult practice. Running at a dead sprint in 90-degree heat on a weekend was something that I was never forced to do, something that the team didn't depend on me to do, but something I knew would allow me to achieve at the highest levels of outdoor track. I thought back to those rainy April afternoons when I had practiced handoffs in the pouring rain, after everyone else had gone inside and decided they'd rather pass up their prac-tice than get soaked. Then I heard the official bark out, "Runners take your marks," so I knelt down in front of my blocks and waited for the set call. My sense of foreboding and fear of failure vanished as the most powerful mental focus I have ever experienced took over. Jolts of adrenaline surged through my veins. I was free of my fear, and my confidence was at its peak. I dug my spikes into the track and placed my feet on the blocks as the official called the runners to the set position. The cheers slowly stopped reverberating in my head, the world froze, my muscles tensed, and the gun sounded.

I exploded out of the blocks and tore into the first curve. I focused on my lane; the beginning of the second curve rapidly dove off the horizon into my field of vision. The straightaway evaporated beneath my feet, and as I approached the curve, I hugged the line, keeping my momentum. The thought never crossed my mind that this was where I had fallen behind in past races. The footsteps of the other runners resounded in my ears, following me, and yet I felt no fear, because I knew that all they would be seeing for the rest of the race was the back of my jer-sey. Coming down the final stretch, I focused on maintaining my form; my coach's mantra of "Knees up, pump your arms!" echoed in my consciousness as I locked my eyes on the second runner, already in position. The figure of my team-mate got larger and larger as I dashed down the straightaway, clinging to the lead despite the pounding footsteps behind me. After what felt like eons, I crossed the finish line and exchanged the baton without incident.

© JIST Works

Although my lungs screamed for oxygen, as I idled down I was able to shout out a booming and hoarse encouragement to my teammate. Two, four, seven runners crossed the zone behind me. As I stumbled off the track onto the infield, my worst fear of bringing my team down was shattered by the triumph of my best run of the year. My team could not have asked for anything more, and I had overcome my mental barriers to turn out my best performance of the year. Not only had I beat other athletes, I had triumphed over myself. That race will forever be emblazoned in my memory as one of the most intense and electric experiences I ever had.

And exactly what has stuck in my mind? The hard work, the determination is what will be with me forever when I think back to our track team. We worked ourselves into the ground all year, and didn't accept anything less. I realize that the reason I got so far is because I worked out harder and longer than most other runners. After that year's season, I found that natural ability has less to do with success than diligence: running on those days when I just wanted to go home and watch TV. After realizing that I had the potential to go so far, those lethargic days occurred less frequently; every day was a stepping-stone toward my ultimate goal of competing with the top runners in the state. Now I cannot and will not be happy with anything less than shattering my old mark and leading another Midland 4X400 team to State Opens in 2003.

—David S., George Washington University

Softball: How Achieving a Goal Made Me Feel

In Ali's own words: "Allow yourself a long period of time to finish your essay, so that you can work through it at your own pace and not feel rushed or pressured. Before you start writing make sure you have a plan or a main guideline written down, so that you will always have something to look at for reference or ideas. After your essay is complete, take a few days off, and then look over it with fresh eyes and critique it as an essay as a whole, to make sure it all fits and flows together. Use your original plan as a checklist to make sure all your main points are clear in your writing and you have answered the essay question fully."

Evaluate a significant experience or achievement that has special meaning to you.

As I joyfully jumped around the infield along with my teammates I was overcome with a great feeling of accomplishment. It was a gray, overcast and humid day in

(continued)

(continued)

the beginning of June, but to the Orange Grove High School girls' softball team it was beautiful. We then gathered in a huddle and waited for our names to be called to accept our medals for winning the 2005 Class S State Championship. I was filled with emotion, and excited that I had contributed to the win. I had started at first base, and I had also driven in the first run of the game. After the game my mom, grandmother and brother were waiting to congratulate me along with a number of my classmates. My teammates and I felt like celebrities, we had our pictures taken, and everyone was clapping and cheering for us. To this day I can still remember the truly incredible feeling I felt after that game. All good things come to an end, and it was time to get back on the bus to go home. Our coach said a few words to us as we pulled out of the parking lot. She told us that she knew how much hard work we had put into our season, and that she was glad that the work we had put in from the March had all been worth it.

It was those words that got me thinking. When I pulled on my white and royal blue uniform, with a royal blue 3 and my last name printed across the back I was one part of a bigger whole. The deep brown clay was freshly lined, and the green grass of the outfield was freshly cut. I stood in the dugout gazing at the field as I felt a tightness come around my stomach like a spider web. But as I strode out to the pitcher's mound, clenching the unmarked ball in my hand, I was calmed by the sea of royal blue around me. The spider web around my stomach released its grip, as I gazed around the field at my teammates. We were all sharing the field, the pressure, the stress and the same common goal. Each one of us made up one part of the Orange Grove team. There was a reason that nine names were penciled into the line up card, because not one of us could achieve our goal alone. Jumping around the field after winning the state championship we were celebrating the success that all of us had achieved together, as a team. Working hard, the Orange Grove team overcame obstacles as a team and not as individuals which led to the achievement of our goal. I had so many memories from the past 10 years of playing softball. Not all of my memories were about my own team.

"Get up, and get the ball!" My mouth dropped open as I stood with my teammates in horror. I looked at the girl next to me, and the girl next to her, blank looks occupied our faces and our mouths hung open. We watched as two girls lay in the outfield crying. "Get up, and get the ball!" The shout of a middle aged man struck again. His navy blue hat sat atop his balding head with the words "Niantic All-Stars" written in italics. His shouts broke the silence, as both fans and players were too horrified to speak. Finally the ball was returned to the infield and the trainer rushed out to the two entangled girls. "One of you needs to call that ball. Nothing like this would ever happen if one of you called the ball. They have the go ahead run on second base, we may lose the game now," he shouted again as he took a few steps out of the dugout. I never saw any coach dismiss an injury in this manner. Applause droned out his screams as the two girls were escorted off the field. The coach went back to where he had been standing and picked up his clipboard as if nothing had happened. I witnessed this event about eight years ago, and I can still remember it clearly. Although winning is the preference, losing is still a possibility. No team can win 100% of the time, which means dealing with a loss is an essential skill. Looking at the positives, even after a loss, is important in order to find the inspiration to try again.

Riding back to Orange Grove, after winning the State Championship, was a moment I had been waiting for and working towards for more than just one season, or school term. This goal had been one of mine for years, and the feeling of accomplishment was as significant to me as the amount of work and practice time I had put in to achieve it.

—Ali M., Stetson University

Running Really Did Change My Life

In Brandon's own words: "The essay is all about saying something important about yourself while displaying your ability at writing a good essay. Brainstorm some things you enjoy doing, then think about why you like them and what they mean to you. When you settle on a topic that you've had some good ideas about, write a draft from the heart! This is just your thoughts on paper; no revising, rethinking, etc. This is all your thoughts on the topic with which you can work. Now, write and revise a draft or two, then get it peer-reviewed as many times as you like. Then ask your favorite English teacher to review it. Take all critique into consideration, but stay true to your theme.

"I had many friends a year ahead of me in school and their essay process taught me a lot. I saw their styles, methods, and successes. From this, I made up my own method. It wasn't so much one piece of advice as it was indirect experience."

I've never ceased being amazed at the changes I've experienced because of one chance event that introduced me to running. Taking up running has altered the very basis of how I see the world. I had never had any interest in running, but one day I was walking with a friend at school when he signed up for cross-country. On the spur of the moment I decided to sign up as well.

In a few short months the first season started, and I had no idea what I had gotten into. Every practice I had to work myself to exhaustion to adapt my body from playing computer games to running five or more miles per day. But it was a pleasant exhaustion which showed the growth I was accomplishing. And as I was growing physically, I found my mind to be strengthening as well. Before I had nothing to drive me. Now, despite the constant fatigue of hard practice, I was growing to love running and the cross-country team with whom I shared this passion. The camaraderie of my fellow runners was infectious, and everyone, no

(continued)

(continued)

matter his background, was happy to share a joke, wait out my cramps, or just be a friend. I persevered, showing up every day of the season, soon graduating from the back end of the 'slow' group to the head of the 'medium' group. I soon found that where I had avoided exercise at all costs, running was now my favorite activity. I loved the strength and dexterity I had gained, the new and interesting friends I had made, and the dedication and open-mindedness I had developed.

Around the same time that I started running, I was introduced to meditation by one of my new friends. Everyday I would meditate, reflecting on the day's events and working to understand how I fit in. I would begin by calming my mind by emptying it of any stress. Once I felt calm, I would examine my actions and thoughts of the day and understand how I think and why I act. As I learned more about Zen meditation, I gained a deeper appreciation for myself, the world, and life. Through meditation, I saw that I could learn to deal with the disappointments in life and better appreciate living my accomplishments and aspirations.

These complimentary skills changed me into a stronger person both mentally and physically. Yet as I began to develop these skills, they started to meld together and change me in different ways. Running had become a form of mediation for me, allowing me to concentrate and reflect under pressure. In turn, sitting mediation taught me a deeper empathy with my mind and body, allowing me to run further and faster because I could better push my limits. As I have grown with these skills, every aspect of my life has become fuller and more enjoyable. Strength of mind and body and the unity of the two have improved my grades and performance in school, started and tightened many friendships, and grown my character. Now practicing running and meditation are integral parts of my character, and I hope to continue developing these skills throughout my life.

—Brandon C., University of Richmond

Essay Theme #5: Leadership and Introspection

Tiny but Most Memorable Experience

In Jaclyn's own words: "I would be sure to get a teacher to review the essay and offer their suggestions. Also, write about something that really means something to you, so that the school can really get a good idea of the type of person you are. Just be sure to make the essay meaningful and not something that the colleges read over and over again. Try to pick something different that they may not have heard before and gives them a good picture of what you are like as a person."

© JIST Works

As on most Wednesday evenings in February, I once again find myself speeding down the snowy hills of the Powder Ridge Ski Resort with several of my eighth grade friends. Our weekly ski trips to Powder Ridge are yet another fraction of the restless, hectic lives my friends and I lead at age thirteen. While skiing, we try to get as many runs in as possible, always racing to the bottom of the slope only to search out the shortest line to deliver us to the peak. Tonight is especially chilly; I can see my warm breath through the cold, dry air, as all the feeling in the tips of my toes quickly begins to cease. It looks as though snow may fall at any given moment.

My friends and I wait excitedly in line at the bottom of the mountain to be carried up the chair lift. When my turn to ride up finally comes, I hastily sit myself down in the green, uncomfortable seat; my feet, confined in bulky ski boots, dangle heavily below me. As we are riding up, the gray clouds finally give in to Mother Nature, and tiny snowflakes begin to glide gracefully through the dark, dull sky. I gaze down upon my navy blue ski jacket, and I notice the most amazing, beautiful thing I have ever laid my eyes on: a perfect snowflake. It is pure white, one hundred percent symmetrical, and gorgeous. This miniature crystal looks so fragile, almost like lace stolen from the dress of an angel.

Suddenly the world seems to stand still, and a sensation of warmth rushes up and down my entire body. For a split second, nothing else seems to matter to me. My entire busy and crazy life just fades away, and I feel an inner peace that I have never experienced before. I begin to see things in a different perspective, no longer distracted by life's trivial matters. I realize that snowflakes this perfect are not created by accident. The snowflake makes me feel as though I have been touched by some greater outside force. I have truly witnessed a miracle, small as it may seem. I feel comforted because I now know that someone out there is watching over me, and I am not alone. A tear slides down my cheek as I watch the tiny snowflake melt into a small puddle on my jacket.

This snowflake has helped create the person I am today. Through observing this tiny wonder, I have become more in tune with the world around me and my own thoughts. Whenever I feel that my life is moving too fast or when life's stresses become almost unbearable, I remember the peace I felt seeing that snowflake on my jacket. Through this perfect snowflake, I realize that at certain moments in life, we can feel God's presence. These moments may last only seconds, but they stay with us forever.

—Jaclyn B., Providence College

Drawing on Leadership Skills in College

In Wes's own words: "Start early and make lots of revisions. Put a lot of time into it and try to meet all the guidelines. When considering the schools to which you'll apply, also start early. Definitely include several reach schools: You want to be an overachiever and shoot for the best."

Describe what you have accomplished in high school.

My high school career has been characterized by both academic (honor roll) and athletic successes. With regard to my work experience, my first paying job outside of my household has been as a cashier at the market in my community. I began working in April of 2004. In addition to my cashiering responsibilities, I also train new staff and work for the owners in their own homes as needed on special projects. During the school year, I work between 10 and 12 hours on weekends only (usually Sunday) because of my varsity running schedules for cross-country and indoor and outdoor track. During the summer months, I work 30-40 hours per week at the local market.

Beginning in the fall of my junior year, I was also hired by the local newspaper, the Town Times, to write a weekly sports column. I cover the cross-country meets as well as indoor and outdoor events. This has given me an opportunity to showcase some of the top achievement of the team. I was elected captain of the cross-country team for my senior year and have worked extremely hard to cultivate the incoming freshmen and provide training and conditioning in the preseason practices I have held since the beginning of August. We have a great team and I believe that in my role as captain I am helping to build more camaraderie through encouraging everyone's best efforts. Our school won the Shoreline Conference XC Championship this fall and three of our runners (myself included) earned All-Conference honors and ran in the State Championship class meet. I was voted by my team for both the MVP and 100% effort awards at our banquet a week ago. In addition, I was named the Benchwarmer Club's Athlete-of-the-Month for my achievements in cross-country in October. I consistently placed in the top one, two, or three places for every race of the 2005 season. Counting my senior year, I have earned eight varsity letters (3 in XC, 2 in indoor track, and 3 in outdoor track).

My volunteer work includes feeding the homeless in New York City as part of a Youth Service Opportunities Project with Rochester Federated Church. I also have run the cross-country/track lemonade stand at each year's agricultural fair to raise money for the school's athletic programs. I have worked for more than 6 years as a volunteer in the town committee's pie and dessert booth each fall.

I have played the trumpet for eight years, four of them as a member of Rochester's concert band. I have participated in five performances (all adjudicated) on high school band trips to Orlando, FL and Virginia Beach.

My educational goal is to acquire an excellent foundation in business management while accumulating credits in marketing as much as possible (perhaps as a minor). I have excelled in my business classes at Rochester High School and believe this would complement a career that combines marketing aptitude in some facet of business that relates to sports management. Just as important, I want to give back to the college community and believe that my leadership strengths and strong sense of commitment to a goal will be an asset to the school. If I am accepted by the University of Hartford, I am committed to working hard and using all of my leadership abilities to personally excel and to help others achieve their goals.

—Wes M., University of Hartford

Confidence-Building: Learning Valuable New Skills

In Kyle's own words: "Start fairly early so that you can talk to people about your essay. Getting several opinions is a good idea and if you start earlier rather than later, you won't feel the time crunch of rushing to get everything done last minute. Pick a topic that will set you apart from other applicants such as a unique experience, or something that no one else will write about. I was also told to pick something which showed a time when I grew as a person."

Describe a significant event in your life.

The word "yes" meant little to me in my childhood. It was merely an answer to a simple question or an acknowledgment of someone speaking to me. That all changed on October 26, 2001. For having shown leadership in and out of school, I was selected to represent my school at the Youth Effectiveness Seminar hosted by Bill Ames. YES had a new impact on my life. Bill Ames came from California to put this three-day leadership seminar on for students at local high schools.

From the moment we entered the Reading library to begin the first day's session, it was clear that we weren't going to be able to separate ourselves by school. Bill desired for us to meet the people of the other schools; consequently, every twenty minutes he would have us get up and find a new seat next to someone we didn't know. Being a bit nervous when I first get to know someone, I found this activity to be a bit uncomfortable at first. However, this was the first step he used to teach us about expanding our "comfort zone," a concept that he kept prevalent throughout the seminar. By doing things that intimidate us, we will eventually become comfortable doing them, which allows us to grow. I have heard this advice in other works such as the movie director Baz Luhrmann's song, when he states, "do one thing every day that scares you." I have concentrated on incorporating this into my life because I am shy by nature, and there is so much more out there for me to experience. To improve teamwork skills, we were given a card with a product and a random prop, and in thirty minutes we had to create a commercial for the product by using our prop. This was the most enjoyable activity of the three days, and we watched our commercial again the next day. For one of the first

(continued)

(continued)

times in my life, I didn't care if I was laughed at because I knew that it was all in good fun. I have learned to lighten up and have a little fun once in a while because laughter is the best medicine to any pains I might have.

Finally, the last activity we did was for one minute to compliment everyone else in attendance. This was the most meaningful activity of the three days to me. My confidence level spiked like my hair on a bad day. From that exercise on, I have been much more self-assured and less nervous when embarking on new experiences. Knowing the importance of his teachings, Bill also insisted that we keep a journal so that in the future we could look back on what we learned and determine how it has affected our lives. I still have that journal, and to this day I do consult it from time to time when things aren't going too well to be able to assess my problems and work out a solution.

Even though only the elite students were selected to this conference, there was still much to learn from it. I have gained several new friends from this experience, and the emotional high present at the end is something that everyone should be able to experience. Although still somewhat shy, I have made great strides in my conversation skills, and because of that I have become friendly with many more people at my school and with people from other schools as well. I have also been able to assess my relationships better as a result of this conference. In addition to assessing them, I can now take steps necessary to correcting the problems that exist. Bill Ames compelled me to look at myself in a different way, and as a result, I have found areas that call for improvement. The process is slow, but with time I have made and will continue to make great strides in my own self-maturation.

—Kyle M., Lafayette College

Leaving Technology Behind on the Coast of Maine

In Kelsey's own words: "Proofreading is key. Write the essay, proofread it yourself, then give it to your parents, then to your teachers, then to… etc., etc., until they can't find anything else wrong with it. Be thick-skinned, and accept constructive criticism. Your English teachers are *very* helpful. I was lucky enough to have an English teacher who used to work as an editor, and a friend whose mother actually worked on an admissions board of a college, going through the application essays. And don't procrastinate. It's stressful enough without it."

© JIST Works

Evaluate a significant experience and its impact on you.

Dense grey fog formed a wall to my left, slowly but steadily rolling in toward the rock spire where I sat. A small island, surrounded by a slick barricade of seaweed covered rocks, vanished into the mist. The outlines of the trees and shrubs gleamed dark and ghostly for a few moments before they, too, were swallowed up. Leaning forward, I watched an otter scamper lightly over the rocks below, its thin, lithe body moving fluidly over the rocks before it slipped into a tidal pool. A cold, brusque wind combed through my hair and streamed through my red fleece jacket, bringing with it the salty brine of the sea.

Two years ago, my family and I took a trip to Maine in early August. We stayed in a little house on Moose Cove for a week. We spent seven wonderful days exploring the rocky shore that formed our front yard and the criss-crossing of dirt roads that made our back yard. We go to Maine every year, but this year's trip was special. In the whole week that we stayed at the cabin, we never saw another person until we drove out to the neighboring town of Trescott.

The solitude of the ocean shore was very peaceful, even though the ocean itself was anything but tranquil or serene. The tides crashed in, the tides roared out, and the waves were wild and untamed at any time of day. I could hear the sound of the waves pounding against the rocks even while inside the house. It was nearly always foggy, with a cold, damp chill and a stiff ocean breeze. For the space of about two hours, the clouds broke and the sun came out, transforming the sky from a stormy grey to a cloudless blue. I sat at the edge of a twenty-foot cliff and watched as waves broke beneath me and sprayed water ten feet above my head. It was thrilling to watch the magnitude of the power of the ocean.

We hiked the Bold Coast trail in Cutler, which took us on a six-mile loop along the cliffs near the Bay of Fundy. In some places, moss hung off the trees in long thin strands. There was one tree that had huge round growths blossoming from the trunk and branches. The last quarter mile of the trail wound on wooden platforms through a bog. Looking off the platforms into the mud, I could see tracks left by moose and deer.

My trip to Moose Cove was an experience that I shall never forget. Without access to telephones, computers, or the Internet, staying in the cottage cut us off from technological influences. Exploring the shore in front of the cottage was like entering a different world. The mist gave the landscape an almost fey look. Ten minutes before we had to leave, we walked out to the wooden chairs overlooking the rocky shore below. The clouds parted, sunlight streamed through, and the seals we'd read about in the guest book but had never seen came out to play on the rocks.

—Kelsey M., Worcester Polytechnic Institute

Optimism, New Perspectives, and Cooking Pasta in Oil

In Todd's own words: "Start early. Application deadlines creep up fast and you need time for teachers to correct it. Write what you feel, not what you think they want to hear."

Crunching on mint lifesavers and watching them spark, eating macaroni boiled in oil, dangling over a pit of lava, and swinging in the trees like a squirrel are some of the highlights from one of my most memorable experiences. During seventh and eighth grade, I was part of a group called IDEAS, made up of kids and a few teachers from neighboring towns. We participated in various diversity and leadership activities; our trip to "Great Hallow Wilderness School" was one of them. After arriving at the camp, I was a little bit uneasy because I didn't really know a lot of the kids from other towns yet. I wasn't sure they would react to the activities the same way I would.

I'm the type of person who likes to be challenged physically and mentally. If I am told that I can't do something, I just want to do it that much more. The first activity we did was called the trust fall where the group stood in a circle with one person in the middle. That person would have to close his eyes, cross his arms over his chest, and just fall with the belief that the people in the circle would not let him hit the ground. We did a variety of trust activities like this along with some group initiatives. Some of the activities were really difficult to figure out mentally and required a lot of planning. Our counselors kept telling us to think outside of normal thought or "outside the box," as they called it, and I tried to do just that. As a result of this experience, I learned not to give up and that if a problem seems impossible that I should step back and go at it from a different angle. I remember the difficulty in trying to fit nine people onto a 1-yard by 1-yard square piece of plywood and being told that we had to do it; otherwise, we couldn't move on to any other activities. After several attempts and careful planning we achieved our goal.

Along with the lessons, I also took home a lot of great memories; the night that two of my group members were in charge of cooking dinner was one of them. We were waiting for dinner. One of the girls, holding onto a bottle of oil, asked how much she should put into the pot. Our counselor, thinking she was referring to the pasta, replied "the whole thing." The next thing I knew the girl in my group proceeded to pour the entire bottle of oil into the boiling water, which we were going to cook our pasta in. We had a good time trying to skim the oil off the top, but the pasta came out all right. The idea behind the camp was to learn to work together and face every challenge with an optimistic point of view. I enjoyed the camp so much because their positive viewpoint defines who I am. The glass is always half full for me no matter what challenge I might be taking on. I know that no matter how much oil I pour in, my pasta will always come out all right!

—Todd M., Bucknell University

© JIST Works

Essay Theme #6: Making a Difference

Mind-Opening Experience: Leaving My Own Little Corner of the World

In Don's own words: "I would tell high school students to definitely start the essay-writing process as soon as their junior year begins, as the revision period takes some time and I believe that this process should be given ample time so as to not create too much stress while ensuring the success and perfection of the essay.

"This process is very important as it is a major part of the admissions process. Besides grades and letters of recommendation, this essay gives admissions officers an idea of who you are as a person, which is essential to securing an acceptance to a university or college. It is a look into the personality of the applicant. Without this essay, admissions officers would judge admittance solely on grades and recommendations by others, never truly understanding the person's personality and desire to learn. This, I believe, is an important and necessary standard for admittance, and as so, it will be another task for high school students to complete before their ascent to college."

Waking up one calm damp morning, I realized that I was truly in Kentucky. As my ears cleared, the distinct echo of our coordinator Alan struck home. Like an impressive grizzly bear attempting to startle intruders on his territory, Alan bellowed his trademark "Good morning people!" By this time, my feet became acclimated to the cold, dirty concrete floor. Satisfied that everyone was finally moving around and filling the vehicles with equipment, Alan sorted out our assigned worksites. Having spent my entire life in a somewhat sheltered middle class world, I wondered how I would react to a church-sponsored trip to Appalachia. Reflecting on where we were headed during the nearly 800 mile trip to the poverty-stricken, sparsely populated county of Owsley in Kentucky, I had plenty of time to ponder how this experience might alter my thinking.

On my first worksite, I met a young mother named Abby, who lived with her husband and their two children. I easily connected with her because I have a cousin who is the same age. With two children in a small trailer without electricity or running water, Abby needed more space. We built a large, square addition on the side of her trailer. All the while, she insisted that we use her parent's facilities even when they were not home. Showing a kind generosity, Abby would not let us leave without ripe, juicy cantaloupes each night. Just being a part of this work was the greatest satisfaction because I knew we were helping others. When the end of the week arrived, a bright sparkle in Abby's eyes was visible as she witnessed the white room that was to be her children's.

(continued)

(continued)

Although I had never been away from home for more than a few days, I was excited to stay nearly two weeks in a part of the country I had never visited. Until I ventured far beyond Rhode Island's borders, I did not understand how the rest of the nation was different. Not only was the Appalachian region new to me, but its people were also very different from my neighbors in Rhode Island. Looking at their lives, I thought that life would be hard and unrewarding for these people, but I quickly learned that they had a certain pride that was unmatched back home. Traveling through the coal-mining heartland of West Virginia and Kentucky, I was taken aback when I noticed how people were willing to risk life and limb by traveling far under the Earth to mine coal with the sole purpose of putting food on their tables. The whole experience shaped my thinking in that I realized I should never prejudge anything. Going into new situations, however daunting, with an open and fresh mind was what I learned in Kentucky, and more importantly what I realized was that people living in difficult circumstances can have much more dignity and generosity than others living in a more privileged environment.

—Don R., Fairfield University

Lasting Impressions from Colombia

Camila's advice appears under the heading of her first essay in this chapter, "Why This School?"

She'll be thrilled. When I tell my mom about this essay she'll squeal and she'll smile she'll be thrilled. The memories will come rushing back; the smell of the kitchen, the folding chairs in the square, the husky man, the thin man, the dark man on the corner with his one-of-a-kind emeralds, the sound of the bolt on the door and the subsiding splashes when someone got home. She'll remember Camillo's macaroons and Gloria's guanava juice and the white steps to the balcony carelessly spattered by anxious feet on their way out of the pool. But if she really thinks about it, she'll remember those footprints were never really a bad thing because if you look down on the way up spotless, white stairs, they all become one giant blur, and if you forget to hold the railing, it's easy to fall...

On the plane to Cartagena, Liz sat with a man who assured her Colombia was safe for her blond haired, blue eyed children—that she would prove wrong all the cousins and parents in Leh-minstuh and Joi-sey who thought she would not return home. I could have told her that. I could have told what my mother had told me about Colombia. I would've said it all resolutely; hiding the shame I felt hearing and sharing their feelings of doubt, knowing that Colombia was more a part of me than the butterflies in my gut. Misgivings produced scrapes, and I felt exposed, my desired identity and my heritage meeting in bitter discord—a mask of acceptable whiteness never having to encounter the troubles of my undetectable "brown" self that emerged only as a convenient bubble on a standardized test.

© JIST Works

After a taxi ride from the airport through the modern city, we entered the walls of Old Cartagena. I expected an adobe surrounded by a termite-ridden fence and overgrown blades of dying grass straight out of "Better Homes and Gardens Magazine" gone bad. I arrived at a Spanish-style building the size of a Boston Brownstone. The middle courtyard had a sparkling pool, no roof, a white floor and three symmetrically placed palm trees beneath a blue sky. It was surrounded by two living rooms, adorned with tables stacked with books overflowing with sophistication. There were five bathrooms, four bedrooms, thriving flora and a dining room table for the five adults and seven kids, all protected in pure, white walls within a fortress within a big, foreign city. I felt like I was living in an MTV Crib.

Daylight in Cartagena meant hiding behind dark shades to evade cries of "mamacita." Night fell and I emerged fully New England, defiantly "popping" my collar to challenge any young woman with her big hoop earrings and seventy year old husband. I was a self-deemed defender of my American life, standing in bitter, conscious resistance to a flurry of Latin strangers in a Starbuck-less square.

Four days being eaten alive by mosquitoes on the Isla del Rosario are better than four days being eaten alive in the city. Smothered in layers of bug spray and sunscreen, I spent those four mornings bronzing on the beach reading about Jackie Robinson for AP U.S. Jackie's tribulations were often interrupted by my own— irritating men scaling the ocean walls selling hideous necklaces. No hablo espanol.

Day two and a familiar four-letter expletive alerted us that *we* were not alone. Dinner marked the beginning of the bitter rivalry. Six blond, something-teen year olds were impatiently blabbering at a table close to ours. Their father Steve strolled in sporting Ray-Bans and that famous yellow band. He pounced after eating, ready to volunteer his life story and achievements: an apartment in New York City, a marina on the Shore, his "Colombian Connections." He elaborated generously about the time he went to Costa Rica and a group of undercover FBI agents tried to sell him an island and cocaine. It was deduced that Steve made his fortune in the drug trafficking business.

We landed in Houston with ease. I sauntered off the plane and indulged in a tall cup of Starbucks and a six-inch sub. As I waited for my flight to Massachusetts, listening to George W's Texas twang on a large screen TV, I shushed Tyler's criticisms to humor any fervent Texan within earshot. Then it hit me: I was just as foreign to Houston, Texas, U.S.A. as I had been to Cartagena, Colombia. I had spent two weeks finding comfort in any thing American; the smell of diner-style waffles on the corner of San Pedro, a dark-skinned waiter tossing our football, my "MTV crib", Steve the trafficker in his "Livestrong." As I resisted the culture and blinded myself to the people who didn't fit the presumed Colombian stereotype, I overlooked one significant detail: Colombia, its people and its history are just as much a part of me as fifty stars, thirteen stripes, purple mountain majesties and a white house. For two weeks I had been a schizophrenic mess, one identity suffocating another, a walking irony: as I hid my Latin roots to evade any association

(continued)

(continued)

with the stereotypes that define the perceptions of the Colombian people, I became the embodiment of the pretentious snob that continues to recognize these stereotypes.

When I get back home, I can tell my friends about the big bad trafficker they knew I would meet in Colombia. When they find out he is from New York, New York, maybe the lines will blur for them too. But like a footprint that has just soiled a spotless white stair, that detail will make everything clear.

—Camila G., Duke University

Essay Theme #7: Music, Literature, and Performing Arts

Piano 101 Cultivated a Work Ethic

In Katharine's own words: "One piece of advice I might offer would be to actually write more than one essay, for the same question/space. I myself wrote three completely different essay drafts (for my 'primary' essay) before finally settling on my final topic (this piano essay). While I would definitely *not* recommend stressing about carrying all of these drafts to the final stages, I found that writing them really helped my thought process. By the time I finalized and submitted my polished essay, I was comfortable that it was as I wanted it; I wasn't still questioning that there was a better topic or expression of my thoughts/ideas/etc."

As I watch my two young piano students bounce eagerly through the front door, I think back to my earliest days as a pianist. Too well I know those nervous eyes and trembling hands that are so easily intimidated by the teacher sitting beside the piano. Once I was that child of eight, afraid to touch the keys lest they make noise, hesitant to take a guess at the notes, lest I be mistaken. Before long, I was a girl of eleven, making myself out to be older but still filled with insecurities. By then I knew I could identify the notes correctly, but still, in touching the keys delicately, I hoped that any mistakes or imperfections would go unnoticed. Today a near adult with stronger fingers and greater confidence, I am no longer afraid to share my interpretation of a composition. When I play, the songs become a musical creation of my own, rather than just a reproduced collection of scales and chords. When I make a mistake, I simply stop to fix it and move on, satisfied with the knowledge that in solving the problem I am only progressing towards the final, polished piece. The genre of the composition is of no matter: my fingers cannot differentiate between styles and know only that the same passion must be

© JIST Works

poured into each note, be it that of a Beethoven Sonata or an Elton John tune. When I am focused on the small black notes harshly juxtaposed to the cold white of the pages, the pressures of daily life ease, even if they do so only fleetingly.

Beginning to play the piano at the age of eight was more a result of my mother's ambitions than my desire to learn an instrument, yet I harbored a certain curiosity. My mother and grandmother were accomplished musicians, and if they could play, I certainly could too. Entering the lesson room for the first time, I had little idea of the number of times I would beg my mother to allow me to give up the piano. Watching my teacher play made it seem so easy; learning it myself was often tedious and frustrating. How could a child of eight have known that aside from learning to read music, one would have to master timing, technique, and theory to become an accomplished pianist.

Through all these years, my mother never once compromised; day after day she convinced me to push through exercises and sonatas. At times I loathed her for it, but today I appreciate her resolution. The self-discipline I developed as a musician carries over into all aspects of my life including academics, athletics, and now the transition into college. Playing the piano has helped me to develop a work ethic, but more importantly it has helped me to understand the importance of performing to the best of my ability in every undertaking. While not every goal in life is easily accomplished, success—be it making money or evoking musical poetry from a keyboard—will come only from perseverance and a desire to continue learning.

—Katharine C., Mount Holyoke College

Base/Basket/Soft(balls)...and All That Jazz

Camila's advice appears under the heading of her first essay in this chapter, "Why This School?"

I have passed, shot, batted, (but mostly kicked) virtually every week of my life since kindergarten. I won my first championship after an undefeated basketball season with the Mystics. I won my last championship in eighth grade, after pitching four innings on the Elmwood Pastry softball team. I have always dreamed of *that* victory, *that* moment; I have always hoped to be *everyone's* rival, on *the* team to beat. In between my first days as a co-ed mite and my current dwindling varsity soccer career, I discovered a niche and found a team that promises *that* feeling. The Hall High School Concert Jazz Band is *the* team to beat, the team with *that* coaching staff, *all* those fans and too many championship rings to fit on two hands. In fourth grade, I began my career as a female trombonist. Last year, I played at Lincoln Center with the fourteen other top jazz bands in the country. No pre-game psych music required.

(continued)

(continued)

Like any other team, we start 0-0. Victory in the end is a result of the hard work that starts with the 45 minutes in school every day and the three hours every Tuesday night and culminates with "Pops and Jazz" time. Every February and March during the weeks that precede this renowned show, we practice 45 minutes during the day, four additional hours three nights a week and eight hours on Sundays. Then for six nights in March, there is madness and our stadium is full and no matter what, we win, because the last chorus of each night prompts confetti, balloons and a standing ovation.

The Hall High Concert Jazz Band has brought a little Miles, Dizzy, Duke and 'Trane to Canada, New York City and Europe. The jazz band has added its own sort of blues, swing and salsa to the Hall Warrior mascot. Mostly, the jazz band has shown a girl a world that exists outside of the shoot, the pass, the tap, the clap, the hush and the clamor in between the lines.

—Camila G., Duke University

Starting a Band: A Lesson in Music, Creativity, and Results from Hard Work

In Matt's own words: "Don't fret too much about it. The essay questions are simpler than you'd expect. I didn't feel like I was being stressed out because of the essay questions, but more because of the entire application process. Be original and write a unique essay. Standing out can be more important than writing a perfect scripted, yet boring, essay."

General Application Essay (The Ohio State University) (200-word limit)

There is one thing that I do that most people would not include on a college application. Freshman year, my friends and I started a band. For over a year we were a struggling garage band that had no future. It can be difficult to pursue something when there is no quick success, but no matter how many people we played for, or how we were received, I always loved playing. When I find something I love, there is no effort too great to help improve it and keep it going. My band experience taught me that if I try hard enough, I can accomplish anything, as cliché as that may sound. We began to write better songs, play more shows, and generate an actual fan base. Because I also love working with computers and designing graphics, I built our band website and designed our logos and CD cover. What I will add to the Ohio State community is someone who is hardworking, creative, and persistent. For something that I love, I will put forth as much effort as I possibly can. I look on my time at college as the chance to pursue my interests, find new things I love, and work hard to fulfill my dreams and goals.

—Matt K., The Ohio State University

© JIST Works

From Being Terrified to Being a Natural: Storytelling and Modern Dance

In Julia's own words: "Be specific; your essay will be much more interesting to read. Don't try to summarize your whole life, use something in particular to demonstrate who you are. Keep your writing clear and concise. Also, be honest; you will come off as a real person rather than some super student."

I am tired of tripping over my own two feet. I want to be graceful, I really do. As we stretch, I flinch in pain, forcing my legs and hips to resemble the other dancers' positions. For years I have yearned to leap nimbly in the air without falling on my face. Sadly, my limbs defy me, arms flopping in all directions and hands creating the dreaded "monster claws." Why do I subject myself to such embarrassment at age seventeen? Even the eight year old can do a split! I balance in a lopsided arabesque, grimacing at my asymmetrical reflection in the mirror. The scuffed white floor seems to give my feet the gift of polarity; they drag along the surface as I fumble through the routine. I am by far the worst in the class, but I don't mind.

Beginning dance reminds me of when I had to perform my first monologue for my acting class at Syracuse University last summer. I had never done a monologue before, and I was terrified. I was already apprehensive about whether I belonged there or not. My passion had always been singing, but I had not had much formal training as an actor. The towering resumes from the other students loomed forebodingly in my head. Free of my shoes, my feet nervously tapped the floor as my teeth chattered. Dee, the instructor, sat against the wall and we flanked him like a panel of judges. I glanced down the row; jiggling knees betrayed anxiety. The others performed and Dee guided them to a second recitation that overflowed with emotion and meaning. Then my turn was called. The room blurred into undefined shapes. I could no longer see faces, only the stark text of the monologue in my head. I attempted to walk confidently to the center of the room. As I recited my monologue to the attentive white wall above the heads of the others, my nerves brutally drove me through the piece at an astounding speed. I finished, breathless and shaking. Dee gently prodded me to do it again, this time with more emotion. Again, I spoke to the wall, trying to make it respond to what I was saying, but not much had changed from my original effort.

When we finished, Dee stood up and announced that it was time to actually entertain each other for a change. Our task was to tell an interesting story. Comfort washed over me; this was a realm where I felt confident. We dispersed to our own spaces and constructed our personal stories. Instead of tense expressions, smiles eased through the room as we thought of familiar tales. Voices buzzed. My feet no longer tapped upon the floor. I thought: I have a funny story. I can make them laugh. I can do this!

(continued)

(continued)

Dee dragged out a bench, its legs whining along the wood floor. It was my turn. I sat on the bench in a casual position, leaning back on my arms. The room was no longer a blend of color and white sound. I saw Maggie, Dee, Desiree, Amy, and all of the others in front of the wall. I was telling them a story. I wanted to reach out to them and make them see the tall reeds sticking straight up from the water on that Florida day. I hoped they would feel my fear as our canoe caught on the water pipe. I wanted them to gasp with terror when my heroic grandfather reached over to help us, tipping his canoe into the alligator-filled marsh. Finally, I hoped my audience would laugh with relief and triumph as my grandfather posed with the canoe, draped in leaves like the Loxahatchee Swamp King. And they did.

So again, here I am diving into another challenge—dance class. Instead of being barefoot in acting class, I am wearing black jazz slippers. But this time, I am not terrified. I don't care whether it takes me one week, or twenty weeks to get the steps. I willingly and happily embarrass myself, waiting until my story appears.

—Julia H., Vassar College

How Music Shapes My Life

This essay resonates with what defines Matt as an individual—and as a student. He draws parallels between his own life and motivation and that of an admired artist. He effectively uses a quote to start the essay and then supports the relevance through links in the content of his essay.

"I think music in itself is healing. It's an explosive expression of humanity. It's something we are all touched by. No matter what culture we're from, everyone loves music." —Billy Joel

Billy Joel, a famous pianist/songwriter, shares my perception of what music really is. His viewpoint is evident in the quote stated above. Many people regard music solely as something they listen to on their way to work or as background noise playing when they're at their job, but music is much more than that. Being a young musician, I can very easily relate to what Billy Joel was talking about when he said this excerpt.

Starting at a very young age, music has always been a huge part of my life. At the age of seven, my mom signed me up for piano lessons from a very strict, yet inspiring teacher, Mrs. Gregory. Music did not mean much to me back then, all I cared about were pogs and playing in my fort outside. Begrudgingly, I practiced everything from Mozart to Dave Matthews, until eventually I found myself actually enjoying the songs I was playing.

Now, at the age of seventeen, I can truly say that I understand what music really is. There are two major aspects of music expressed in Billy Joel's quote, those being self-expression and the ability to heal. Many people might not realize this, but music can help individuals forget their problems and just relax. Music comes from many places, but mainly the heart, that's why so many people are touched by it. I started playing acoustic guitar two years ago and haven't missed a day since. I do not know what I would do without it because it gives me a lot of inner happiness. Whenever I'm by myself or with my friends, the guitar always finds a way to put us in better, livelier moods. In this way, music is healing.

My mood usually dictates the songs I play. My family and friends can easily guess my thoughts and feelings just by listening to how I play and the music I select. Many famous composers and songwriters' music also reflected their emotions. For example, Bach's more loud and explosive songs were written when he found out he was going blind. Music can be an expression of a person's soul.

I'm certain music will always remain an important part of my life. It defines who I am in so many ways because it comes from my heart. Not only does it express how I am feeling, but also by playing, I am able to bring happiness to others. Like Billy Joel, music fills all the gaps in my life. It is often the sole expression of how I am feeling. Billy Joel and I are very much like many others in this world, without music, our lives would not be complete.

—Matt B., University of Connecticut

An Essay on Romanticism (C Block English)

In Christina's own words: "The school I'm attending required that you send an essay that you already had written in high school, so I feel that it is important to take all the essays you are writing in your junior and senior years very seriously because they could potentially help you get into college.

"After writing an essay for the other schools I applied to, I feel as though the best advice I could give would be to *show* who you are as opposed to telling all about yourself. Don't just tell the reader of your essay that you are a leader; show that you are a leader in the writing. Share something unique that sets you apart from other people or something that you are passionate about that brings out your character."

The period of romanticism was a time in which literature was explored in new and more inspiring ways. The literature written by many profound authors during this generation incorporated the ideas of moral uncertainty, freedom, corruption, and sometimes death. The three most important elements that make a story or poem romantic are the involvement of nature as being benevolent and powerful,

(continued)

© JIST Works

(continued)

the ideas of the supernatural, and the fascination with the darkness of the gothic past. With the incorporation of these elements, a piece of literature can truly be considered romantic.

The use of truth and understanding residing in nature in a piece of literature accurately represents the style of romanticism. In looking at literature throughout the romantic time period, "Thanatopsis" by William Cullen Bryant is a prime example of nature prevailing and providing wisdom to the audience. In an excerpt of the poem, nature says that "Yet not to thine eternal resting place/ Shall thou retire alone, nor couldst thou wish/ Couch more magnificent." (31–33) Bryant continues to write that when man dies, he will go away in nature with the best and one will be living among the "pensive quietness" and "venerable woods." Nature takes on these personal qualities to point out that death is a natural thing for all humans and needs to be accepted by man. The truth of death dwells in the force of nature. Along with the idea of death and nature related, "The Tide Rises, The Tide Falls" by Henry Wadsworth Longfellow highlights nature with the use of tides representing time in nature. Nature is endless and timeless. Man dies and fades away from life insignificantly because the waves "efface the footprints in the sands" while the tide continues to rise and fall in every life. Nature is benevolent in the poem "The Rhodora" by Ralph Waldo Emerson because it suggests that things in nature simply exist because they are beautiful. Man asks nature questions on its reasoning for existing, and nature answers, "Beauty is its own excuse for being" (12), suggesting beauty exists because it is pure and pretty and a divine power brings us closer to the Rhodora. The idea of something beautiful in nature bringing one closer to divinity enhances the concept of the over soul: the relationship between man, God, and nature. The way man believes he can reach an understanding of something is through nature, intuition, and with the assistance of God. The use of nature in stories and anecdotes written by Henry David Thoreau endorses the ideas relevant in romanticism. It further defines nature as a form of language. Throughout Thoreau's literature, he points out nature as a source of protection above all other things. In his story, "Walden", he speaks of going to the wilderness and shows that through nature one can learn the truths about oneself and better understanding it. Ralph Waldo Emerson, in his writing of "Nature", explains the idea in romanticism that God is good and God works through nature. He also says that man is capable of evil but through trusting ourselves man can realize that he is part of the Divine Soul source of all good in nature. These ideas of nature evident throughout the literature of the romantic period add to the significance and importance of their existence in the writings during this era.

The exploration of the supernatural in literature defines certain beliefs of the time in romanticism. Nathaniel Hawthorne's "Rappaccini's Daughter" portrays the things above normal science and understanding. The idea of Beatrice, who is in immortal, touching someone and causing them to wither or die, is beyond the normal realm of nature. The concept of having a poisonous plant that possesses the power of killing someone or Rappaccini's invention of an immortalizing potion is used in Hawthorne's story to bring out the imagination and creativity to his literature. The conception of the supernatural in his work enhances his intricate plot line and adds to this fascination during the romantic period of searching deep into the imagination of one's own mind and in others. Romanticism consists of this notion of rising above the "dull realities" of life and exploring exotic settings in a higher sense to reveal underlying truths. One can understand this belief with the use of the supernatural because Hawthorne takes reality to the next level with Rappaccini's corrupt way of controlling his daughter through his poison and the doctor convincing Giovanni to use the potion. It reveals the truths behind evilness and spitefulness. Washington Irving, the author if "Rip Van Winkle" is also able to incorporate this idea with his character of Rip, who unnaturally sleeps for twenty years. This use of the supernatural emphasizes that a change in life after a long period of time can bring a better understanding to living life.

The fascination of the gothic past is important to this era, for it encompasses the works of some of the most famous authors and adds to the darker side of romanticism. Edgar Allan Poe, an author who sought to venture in the mystical realm of senses, reveals the significance of the gothic past in his story of the "Masque of Red Death." This idea of mystery is apparent in this story because death appears behind this masque, symbolizing the plague that is occurring outside this wondrous castle. Tension happens in the house at the ring of the clock every hour and raises the ideas of the reality that time is moving on as they are having fun in this world they believe will never end. It also arouses fear among they people since they do no know what will happen to them next. There is this mystical, gothic setting, in which there are different colored rooms. The last one is black with red curtains and the ticking clock that contributes to the idea of the unknown and fearfulness of the guests is in this deathly colored room. Edgar Allan Poe was able to incorporate his portrayal of gothic tradition to add to the terror and suspense of his short stories. He uses that to bring out the masterful truth that lies in the dark and irrational pits of the human mind. Nathanial Hawthorne, much like Poe, indulged himself in the darkness of the gothic past. His story, "The Minister's Black Veil", introduces a wicked manner of sin in everyone's life. Because the character of Mr. Hooper wears a veil that covers his entire face, might reveal that he's trying to make his people aware of the significance of sin in their life. By doing this, he sets up this mystical uncertainty among the people who become fearful of him because he won't reveal his face. This story, with the use of the gothic style, reflects romanticism because it brings out the truth in life that whether people are aware of it or not, they are secret sinners in their lives. It also brings out that people of the time would rather speculate on the mystery of Hooper's sanity as opposed to confronting this idea of sinful behavior within their own lives.

The most important elements of romantic literature, the involvement of nature, the exploring of the supernatural, and the fascination with the gothic past, are the

(continued)

(continued)

leading factors of classifying a piece of literature as being romantic. Authors of the romantic period use these concepts interchangeably in their poems and stories to create meaning and understanding of the time period. Their works enhance the romantic sensibility of seeking to rise above the normal branch of life and searching for a deeper meaning behind truth, death, life, freedom, and much more.

—Christina G., Wheelock College

Essay Theme #8: Who Am I?

A Creative Way of Describing Unique Attributes

In Vickie's own words: "There are a few different approaches to the essay-writing process. Many people write a very standard 'look at how this situation changed my perspective on life' essay. If you decide to go the life-changing event route, it needs to be an event from high school, preferably from the second half. You need to find an interesting spin to distinguish yourself from the crowd. Be specific, with details that truly establish the event in a reader's mind.

"If you haven't had an interesting life-changing event, try discussing a leadership position or an interest of yours that blossomed into something bigger to show what makes you tick. Above all, be yourself! Show your true personality; don't attempt to sound like someone whom you consider to be more interesting or important than you. You'll end up sounding fake. The aim is to make yourself memorable, and if you write a generic essay, you will get lost in the crowd."

Tired of Barbies? Sick of G.I. Joe? Your dog chewed off the head of your favorite Batman toy? Well, then, try one of the new Vickey A. action figures! This product has been around for almost eighteen years, and it's coming to a college campus near you! Here's a sampling of the different Vickey dolls offered on the market now:

Latin Scholar Vickey comes wearing a shirt stating "Puellae Regunt," meaning "Girls Rule." Open up her backpack to find a Latin/English dictionary, Edith Hamilton's Mythology, and Ovid's The Metamorphoses. Press the button on her back and hear her quip, "Amo linguam Latinam" (I love Latin) and "Volo esse magistram Latinam" (I want to be a Latin teacher).

172

When football and basketball season comes around, pick up Pep Band Captain Vickey. If you need some pep, Vickey can supply you with boundless energy! Let Vickey teach you all of the standard cheers—she loves getting everyone into the game! Captain Vickey comes with tenor saxophone, clarinet, and folder of pep band music. Deck her out in wacky costumes for the pep band themes, such as Toga Night and Super Hero Night!

Don't forget about Runner Vickey. Lace those running shoes onto her feet and let her run for the Beaufort's Lady Tigers track team! She comes with practice outfit and ill-fitting uniform. Hear Vickey cheer for her teammates when you raise her fist over her head! At the end of the season, give her the 100% Award for always trying her hardest, even if she is the slowest member of the team.

Need a snazzy outfit for next week's party? Turn to Tailor Vickey! With a tape measure draped around her neck and a pin cushion in her hand, Tailor Vickey can cut, sew, and embroider herself a whole new wardrobe! With a quick snip and a bit of thread, she can make an oversized shirt fit like a glove. You can even design a new pattern for Vickey to try out on her trusty sewing machine. And get this— Tailor Vickey can make accessories, too! Check out her handmade denim bag!

Singer/Songwriter Vickey dreams of a successful career in the music business one day. Have her play her guitar—she has real strumming action! Along with her guitar, Vickey comes with her song notebook. Inside you can record all of her lyrical inspirations. Carry it around with you all the time—you never know when inspiration will hit! Help Vickey on her way to being a star!

There are many, many more Vickey A. action figures, representing all the aspects of the real Vickey A. Vickey dolls are not sold separately and can currently only be found in Beaufort, South Carolina. Pick up your very own set of Vickey dolls today!

—Vickey A., University of Richmond

Changed by a Sport, a Team, and a Coach

Meghan's advice appears under the heading of her first essay in this chapter, "Influential Person."

A. Think back to what you were like as a student and as a person in your first year of high school. Consider yourself now. Tell us how you have changed, and why. We are more interested in learning about how you have changed or grown as a result of an experience rather than the details of the experience itself.

I nervously enter the crowded halls of Hall High School as my eighth grade seniority quickly becomes a memory. My confidence decreases with each step I take.

(continued)

(continued)

I walk around the gathered cliques of upperclassmen and advance towards the freshman wing. I avoid eye contact, but catch quick glimpses of my new schoolmates. I am immediately envious of how comfortable they are in a school that is unfamiliar to me. I climb the stairs and I find all my friends, they are no longer eighth graders, but freshmen.

Beginning my first year in high school I was unsure of my new surroundings. I had difficulty adjusting both scholastically and socially. In middle school teachers would change test days and homework assignments at a class's request. In high school I found myself having multiple tests on one day. Through the difficult transition I adjusted to my surroundings by immersing myself in school activities and familiarizing myself with both the upperclassmen and the school. After my freshman year I still found myself in awe of the upperclassmen around whom I was privileged to be. However, I was no longer scared. One senior whom I had befriended during soccer asked me why I didn't do track, and I covered up my fear with an excuse about having to baby-sit my sisters. She didn't buy my excuse and made me promise to be a member of the track team. I smiled and agreed half-heartedly, never expecting to follow through on a promise that would forever change the path of my high school career and the person that I have become.

Hesitantly walking down the hall toward the gym, I anticipate a disastrous first track practice. Having had no running experience besides the standard mile testing, I already feel anxious about how I will run compared to others with more experience. I look out the frost-covered windows at the snow painting the ground, and try to grasp the idea of why anyone would voluntarily run in such cold conditions. My doubts are extinguished when I see my spirited new coach Donald O'Connell. He greets me by name despite the fact that I have never been on the team before. Coach O'Connell is not your standard track coach in sweatpants; he dons shorts and a lightweight coat during the most frigid weather and wears socks on his hands in lieu of gloves. From an initial meeting it is apparent that he is a free spirit. A stranger to Hall High School's running program may believe he is crazy and could possibly shy away from track, but any member of our division will attest to Hall's envied running program. Knowing of the reputable team and of Coach O'Connell's hard work and love of the team, I know that with guidance and encouragement joining track will be something I would never regret. With a hint of optimism, I drop my backpack and go down to the locker room to change.

After a few weeks of rigorous training, I begin to realize why the track team has such a large crowd. Unlike most coaches, Coach O'Connell does not yell at you to run faster, he encourages you to "go to the well" and to try your hardest. Coach O'Connell emphasizes a runner's importance to the team but allows you to run for self-improvement. For the first few weeks of practice I find myself in the back of the group, but that encourages me to improve and live up to the team's standards. In the beginning of the season I try to run with my friends, but none of them seem to run my pace. I am scared to run by myself, but I begin to run with other girls who run a similar pace to me. As a result I am more confident running

© JIST Works

because I am with a group. Also, after having most of the school watch me run when I am sweating and breathing heavily, I find myself not to be so shy around my classmates. I realize that everyone on the team has been through the same experience and is more concerned with themselves than with my performance. As teammates we develop a special bond between upper and lower classmen alike.

As an underclassman I sought guidance from the experienced upperclassmen, yet now as an upperclassman I have assumed that role. During lunch I find myself talking with different people outside of my group of friends. I am involved in a wide array of clubs, and I finally feel like a member of the school community more so than I had been before track. The strange hallways seem welcoming. Even my classrooms are inviting and I find myself more willing to seek out help from my teachers rather than sitting in class confused. I am no longer the silent girl in the class who only speaks when called upon, but I am an active member in all my classes. Track gave me the skills that have opened many doors for me now in the present but will also in the future, to be independent and to overcome my fears.

The cheers of the fans echo through the arena as heat 1 takes off at the sound of the gun. I stand shaking near the starting line, doing quick stretches as I prepare to begin my race. The sprinters round the final corner and begin the last straight away. The coaches shout times to their tired runners, the parents shout encouragement, and I repeatedly mumble "I can do it" to myself repeatedly to eliminate my thoughts of running towards the door.

Track gave me the skills to conquer tough situations in all areas of my life. Rather than abandoning a tough homework assignment, I stay on it until I finally have some understanding of it. Each race that I run has a finish line and no matter how far away it seems or how impossible, I always make it to the end. I apply this to my life even when I am not running. I have more focus, I see the finish line and have that mindset when staying up late to finish an assignment. I know that the work that I put in will be what I get out of it. In track you have to practice and work towards your goal, and in life I know that I cannot just breeze by without getting anything done. In middle school I would do what I needed to do, nothing more, but now I know I cannot succeed by doing the bare minimum. When you work hard towards your goal, anything can be achieved if you put forth the effort. After doing Physics practice problems for hours on end, I feel more prepared for the test than if I had gone to sleep. After each track practice I have such a sense of purpose and satisfaction, and I know that I want to have this feeling in everything to which I apply myself to in life.

I walk through the doors of Hall High School and stuff my keys in my purse. I greet my fellow classmates and walk past a large crowd gathered in the middle of the hallway. I wave at a few underclassmen whom I have not seen all summer and watch freshmen make their way through the crowded hallway. I proceed to the senior wing, and realize that next year at this time I will once again be a freshman.

—Meghan H., James Madison University

Why Engineering? Why This College?

In Dan's own words: "Be truthful. That's important. Go to the Web sites of the colleges of interest to see what they are looking for—is this really you? Can you envision yourself at this school?"

What has influenced your selection of a major?

Since my sophomore year in high school, I have known that I want to pursue engineering as a major in college; the University of Hartford's mechanical and civil engineering programs are of particular interest. During October, I had an opportunity to visit the campus with my twin brother (also applying) and was impressed with not only what I learned about the program but the beautiful campus and surrounding community. I also had an opportunity to meet with Coach Manizza; I am very interested in participating on both the indoor and outdoor track teams. I began to sense that this was the right environment for me, a small college atmosphere offering the academic and athletic benefits of a large university. I believe this is a school where I can pursue my academic studies and prepare to ultimately realize my professional goals.

During the summer, I had an opportunity to spend a day shadowing an engineering vice president at Pratt and Whitney to look at the way a real airplane engine is built and to observe the engineers who design them. "This is just like what I used to do as a little kid when I was building model cars," is what I thought to myself as I was walking around the production line of one of the new engines being made. I could envision myself possibly working at Pratt & Whitney designing aircraft engines someday. I saw the engine in every stage of its creation and was fascinated at the similarities of what I did with models and what they do with steel and other composites.

Before discovering mechanical engineering, I was also interested in civil engineering. I went to Yale University to talk to the overall project manager for a $45 million dormitory renovation for a day this summer. She is employed by Daniel O'Connells, the general contractor. I toured the dorm that was being renovated and had an opportunity to talk to a civil engineer and meet one of the project interns. I was able to get a good understanding of the difference between field work as an on-site engineer and the more administrative responsibilities of a general contractor or project manager. I could once again see myself possibly working as an engineer on such projects.

Both of these experiences helped me to finalize my academic goal of pursuing engineering as my major—either mechanical or civil. Knowing the reputation the University of Hartford has and believing that I can contribute as a student in the engineering program has helped me to know that my decision to pursue early action admission at U-Hartford is a sound one. From all of my research and my two campus visits, U-Hartford emerged many months ago as one of my top choices for pursuing my education if I am selected for admission.

—Dan M., University of Hartford

© JIST Works

Bridging Two Cultures, Two Homes

In Stephanie's own words: "Start early; the more time you have the better! Have your English teacher look over your essay, especially with grammar and any suggestions that he/she might have—taking College Writing really helped me out with my essay. Before you start writing look at what the applications are asking for, and see if you can write about a topic of your choice, and then see if you can use it (or some form of it) for all your applications.

"The most helpful pointers that I got from my College Writing class were to realize that you must convey something about yourself that you would like the admissions office to know. Use the story or incident that you are telling to convey what type of person you are, and hence what you can offer the college. The college essay is used not because the Admission Office wants to know about the time you broke your leg, or about my family in Italy, but how that story reflects your character and what kind of person you are. If the college asks for a specific question, because some do, make sure you stay on point."

However cliché the saying may be, the hardships in my life which I have learned to overcome relate to the phrase that the grass is always greener on the other side. Throughout the past seventeen years of my life, I have struggled with the despair of being in a constant state of division. I was torn between the life that my parents have established for themselves here in America, and my heritage and family across the Atlantic in Italy. While I am here in America, enjoying the benefits of my education and the company of my friends, I cry for my family and long for the "Italian way of life" which is so deeply rooted within me. While I am in Italy, I find myself acknowledging and understanding the fact that I have endless opportunities awaiting me in America.

My childhood memories consist of my brother and me racing through my grandfather's gardens and into the *piazza*, where our friends and neighbors greeted us with wide smiles and warm hugs. Jovial conversation resonated throughout the square as my family and friends sipped their espresso and exchanged stories, laughter, and advice. As I grew older, I began to understand that the community of that small Italian town served as more than a gathering of friendly faces, but also as a tool in my growth. The community's uninhibited flow of love and concern for one another has instilled in me the importance of acceptance and embracing the positive attributes of each individual. When I returned to America seeking these same qualities from my community, I became distraught when I was met with reserved cliques that seemed to be focused solely on their own personal matters and agendas.

(continued)

(continued)

Yet, when I applied the optimism and positive outlook that I had adapted from my Italian environment, I found that these "agendas" were driven by self-motivation and the aspirations to achieve the coveted American Dream. My parents, who moved to this country with nothing but self-determination, perseverance, and a hard-work ethic, serve as a prime example of America's ability to allow one to grow from rags to riches. It is that fortitude and resolve that has been evident in every aspect of my life—from academics to soccer—that has been a source for the success that I have achieved thus far. I was also aware that with this same work ethic, paired with the goal-driven atmosphere of our country, opportunities for continued success would be bountiful.

Eventually, I came to realize that I would have to accept that the situation would never change, and the distance between my two homes would never shorten. Instead, I have learned to bridge this distance by incorporating the positive attributes that I have attained from both countries into my daily routine, and I now live my life by this resulting philosophy. Stepping back from the despair that the feelings of being torn provided, I have come to understand that I am exceptionally lucky to be blessed with the opportunity to experience the best of both worlds. This experience is not only enriching, but also serves as an instrument for me to live my life by my maximum ability; utilizing my community- and family-based ambitions as well as my eagerness and resolve to succeed. Although the pains of distance still periodically take effect of me, I have learned to view the bigger picture with the gratitude and optimism that now dominate each aspect of my life.

—Stephanie C., Fordham University

Love of Learning and Life Leads to Changes in College Selections

In Matthew's own words: "Use a teacher mentor or English teacher to help edit your writing before sending your essay in with the application. Use different essays if necessary and it helps to understand the characteristics of a specific university and apply that into your writing. For example, if it is a religious private school focus, you may focus on those aspects, or the diversity of a school, or even on the location or special programs that it may offer and how you would use this to your advantage. You can also use a personal experience to better express yourself.

© JIST Works

"I had a unique experience by attending St. Bonaventure University for two years, while for one semester attending American University for a special program. Attending another institution made me want to transfer even more—and it also improved my writing skills. Therefore, after my second year of college, I transferred to my present institution at UMBC; I transferred there because of location and size and the diversity that it offered. I also considered my anticipated career after college (currently majoring in history and political science), the opportunity to be so close to Washington, D.C., and the reputation that UMBC has in getting their undergrads into good graduate schools (another one of my goals)."

Many things have led me to where I am today, and many of the experiences and events that occurred so far in my life have changed me. However, I see every experience, every event, and every struggle or doubt I once had has made me grow in character and has pointed me closer to my final destination.

I understand and comprehend things that I never thought I would before due to many experiences in my life. Up until the near end high school, it seems that I may have understood not much at all. Life seems to suddenly smack you in the face, saying "hello," and slowly things come back into focus and real learning begins. One of my first great experiences of my life was a trip to Kentucky like Habitat for Humanity, but as a local event for my home town. This certainly opened eyes and made me understand more of what is important in life, as well as what is not. Then there is college, certainly a life altering experience for anyone, where a different kind of learning ensues—where issues and topics that I once never gave an opinion or thought, became the forefront of curriculum and discussion in class. Now, I am abroad from my home school in Washington, DC, for only the second time in my life studying and doing the things that have become my career goals in American University's Washington Semester Program. By studying, listening to speakers, working at MIT Washington Office as an intern, and being able to go out into DC and attend these round table and committee meetings with the people I wish to work for in the future only extend my motivation to become something better than I really am.

A big smack in the face is what I call this. I have been experiencing and doing more in the past two years of my life, than my entire lifespan. I love to live and learn, and I can only wonder where my life leads me next.

—Matthew P., University of Maryland–Baltimore County

Essay Theme #9: Challenges, Accomplishments, and New Adventures

From Germany to Studying in the United States: True Cultural Studies

In Veronika's own words: "When I had to write the letter of motivation for my application to study in the United States, I thought about the question why I was suitable for this rare place in the exchange program for several days. So the actual point why I thought and still think I am suitable for this is because I want to take the challenge and the academic benefits that I get out of it. I was aware that it might be hard and complicated sometimes but the decision to do it is important.

"So my advice for high school students is that you should really write about yourself, about your passions and your decision to go along with all the obstacles that might appear in order to take the challenge and grow with it. Furthermore, education is far too important to mess with it and after a wholehearted decision on a college you should give your best to convince the people reading it with your honest view on the reasons why you want to go to this particular college. In my opinion it is okay to sell oneself in a good light but also to be honest about it and the activities you are doing. The personality and the purposefulness out of a passion should be enough to convince the office of admission instead of writing your life new with a great lack of actual connection to the real life. So think what you can do, think why you want to do something and if you have a passion, an aim or a dream, those are the things that count and not only what sounds good on a resume."

Please state the reason for your intended study abroad.

The most important reason for my intended study abroad is to benefit from the courses at Wesleyan University which are relevant for my field of study. I chose a selection of very interesting courses from the catalogue to fulfill the demands of my majors of American Studies and Compared European Ethnology. Wesleyan's American Studies are an interdisciplinary program and integrate subjects from different fields of study. Especially the integration of anthropology and American Cultural Studies offer me a great opportunity to combine my two subjects in courses like Anthropology of US Cities. On the one hand the course provides a "focus on understanding power and inequality in post WWII American cities" to enhance

© JIST Works

my education in American Studies and on the other hand I can profit from the use of Cultural Anthropology, a method which is relatively new and therefore still less used in Compared European Ethnology. I am really willing to use the chance of learning and living in the USA as a student and profit from the university courses as well as from the experience these two semesters would offer me.

Besides my academic motivation there are of course personal reasons for my intended study in the USA. I am convinced that it is essential for a student of American Studies to study or work in the USA for at least two semesters. There is no other way to get to know the people, understand the varieties of culture and learn the language and its idioms. Understanding a country and its culture is more than learning theories out of books, it is a feeling you only develop from living and breathing in that country. The USA is such a big country and there is so much to experience in so many ways that I would feel very lucky if I was given the opportunity to study in the USA.

I am conscious about the responsibility I have to deal with and I am aware of the problems I will have to face. It will not be easy to study in a foreign country but often one can learn a lot from unpredictable situations. As a conclusion, I want to say that the best reason for my qualification for my intended study abroad is my wholehearted intention to use the chance of two semesters in the USA in every possible way.

—Veronika H., Wesleyan University

Achieving Eagle Scout: Much More Than a Badge

In Brett's own words: "Write about something true to your heart that helped you grow and mature as a person. It makes no sense to write on something that has no emotional impact for you. Personal experiences that are full of true heart help. Chances are if the topic is reasonable enough, you can relate a personal experience to it. That way, the writing becomes less painful to accomplish."

The sun hovered over the panoramic canvas of clouds on a brisk Sunday morning in November. My limbs surged with excitement as flocks of townspeople staggered down to the church parking lot. Splitting the masses of bundled faces and winter coats, a group of scouts in earth-tone uniforms gathered before me with a smile. After everyone raised his camera, the Reverend, a preacher with a bubbly personality, wedged himself between me and my best friend. He silenced the crowd and immediately began an elaborate speech: "We are gathered here today

(continued)

(continued)

to bless this new gift for our community, which could have not been possible without..." This was a moment to remember. Not just by me, but the whole town. Thunderous applause had immediately followed the Reverend's remarks. After eleven years of being a part of this town, I was finally able to give something back to my humble community, and in return, I would receive a badge that represents the highest rank possible, Eagle Scout.

My goal was by far no easy task. Through hard work and perseverance, I learned that there's more to a badge than just red, white, and blue fabric woven tightly together. It is a reward that illustrates character and honor, but best of all, it represents the overwhelming appreciation a person receives from the community. If a person does something unique to earn that badge, it becomes an everlasting memory. But what would I do that would make a positive impact on the community?

The search began with leaders hinting at "barely passing" projects such as bat feeders and painting a fence, but taking the easy route wouldn't build my pride. What good is a badge if I did the bare minimum to earn it? I needed ambitious ideas.

But soon my brain ran dry of ideas. Then during a campout as I was gazing into the radiant fire with discouragement, one of my leaders came up to me with a concerned tone of voice. "You've come too far to quit now, Brett. I know you are having trouble deciding, but I can make a suggestion..." It is a project that gives back to the church that has supported our group for many years, but which never asked or received anything for its patronage. An idea sparked: a pavilion would be perfect, a place where Sunday school classes and other gatherings could be held.

I told my father about the project, and he explained to me just how much work it would be: fundraising, planning and zoning regulations, town meetings, building codes, architectural drawings, material lists, building inspections, excavation equipment, trucks, and power tools were all pieces to this puzzle that would have to be put together. I felt as if I had been run over by an 18-wheeler. I never sank so low so fast. Then my Dad looked at me with a grimace. "You can do this, Brett; I know it. All you need is perseverance." A couple of months went by, forms were filled out, and I made several phone calls to just about every lumber company in the state. All that was left was to assemble a crew to bind the pieces together.

I turned to local volunteers for help, but many were too involved with their lives to lend a hand. This shut a door in my face. Now that there was no way out, I needed to find a window. Leave it to the tied and true scouts and scoutmasters I've grown up with to be the cavalry. Within four arduous weekends the building was erected. My pavilion had no longer been my own project. We had completed it as a team because we both yearned for that sense of fulfillment. That badge now epitomized more than it ever meant to me. It now was defined by the hard

© JIST Works

work and endurance that created the pavilion. I may not be with my troop when I enter my adult life, but I will know that the scouts will always be with me because there's more to a badge than woven fabric: there's a story hidden between each colorful thread.

—Brett W., Rochester Institute of Technology

Volleyball Plus a Hurricane—Unlikely Formula for Bonding

In Megan's own words: "Let the essay show who you are as a person. You want the reader to remember your essay, so be unique. The most important part of your essay is the beginning because you don't want them to read the first paragraph and get bored."

We were the last two of our group left in the pool as the wind began to swarm above us, making each palm tree move chaotically. There were about twenty other people outside with us, but we knew it was going to become dangerous quickly so we decided to leave. We reluctantly climbed the stairs and ran for the warmth of our towels. Teeth chattering and tightly wrapped up in our white hotel room towels, we scooped up our clothes and slid on our flip-flops. As Heather and I walked towards our hotel room we heard the shrill sound of the lifeguard's whistle calling for everyone to get out of the pool. It was closing because Hurricane Frances was about to hit Walt Disney World in Orlando, Florida.

Back in our hotel room, after showering off the chlorine, my two coaches, my twelve other teammates, and I huddled into one of our rooms for a meeting. Coach Hanner explained to us that we should take our meal tickets and collect as much food as we could from the cafeteria since no one knew how long lock-down would last.

By the time we were ready to go down to the cafeteria it was pouring rain and the wind had strewn palm tree leaves all across the soggy grass. We carefully made our way to the cafeteria, dodging puddles and taking precaution not to slip on the pool deck. We arrived to find the cafeteria was swamped with other teams and families. The noise bounced off the walls as a sea of wet rain coats pushed their way through the crowd to get their needed food. We purchased our grilled cheeses, Uncrustables, and Dasanis and puddle-hopped our way back to our hotel rooms prepared for what we didn't know would be one of the most memorable nights of our lives.

(continued)

(continued)

Our team was divided into two pairs of adjoining rooms to go into lock-down, each one with a coach and a parent. Since it was still the beginning of the season my group decided that instead of starting on our homework right away we would have some team bonding time. Our coach taught us some games and we quickly forgot about the hurricane just on the other side of the wall. The only thing that reminded us about it was the mattress propped up against the window to prevent anything that might come through it from hitting us. Throughout the evening, the phone rang incessantly with worried parents on the other end, wanting to know if we were alright. With every call we received, the fear in the room swelled like the giant storm outside. Around ten o'clock we were all tired from waking up at six that morning and playing an intense day of volleyball (we even managed to take on all three mountains in the Magic Kingdom). We knew that if we fell asleep soon we wouldn't be able to worry about the hurricane, so we drifted off to sleep as the wind continued to demolish the grounds.

I awoke the next morning to find that the wind had become even fiercer; it sounded like we were traveling down the runway, just before the plane left the ground. I took my Disney Princess blanket and sleepily stumbled into the adjoining room where the rest of my group was watching <u>Mulan</u> on the Disney movie channel. We spent the rest of the day comforting each other so that we could try to forget about the storm. We tried to focus on what the next day's endeavors would bring us.

At six o'clock that night, lock-down ended. A year earlier, when we started planning our Disney Volleyball Tournament, no one would have guessed that we would have had to endure a hurricane, but not only did we improve our volleyball potential, we also made lasting friendships and bonded as a team.

—Megan S., Furman University

A Man of "New Cheese"—a Wonderful Turnaround Story

In Brandon's own words: "Write about something important to you, something you feel deeply about, and be honest, but not too revealing. Then rewrite as many times with as much input as possible and from as many sources as you can. It will help an essay become well-rounded for many different readers."

© JIST Works

One piece of literature that had an extraordinary influence on me and assisted my understanding of certain events of my past experiences is called <u>Who Moved My Cheese</u>, by Spencer Johnson M.D. The content of the book focuses on change, and change is a word that can very clearly describe my life. The word cheese in this book is simply a metaphor for life, goals in life, and happiness, which are ever fluctuating. This book focuses on adapting to change, instinctively and mentally. In a sense I could say that I switched from cheese to cheese, from happiness to happiness, in order to find my true self; I was completely unaware of whom I was. All this confusion caused me to make mistakes repeatedly. After making drastic changes in my lifestyle, I discovered my greatness, intellectual potential, personal drive, and desire to learn. Changing may have fixed some of my faults, which I do not regret once having, I simply appreciate what I learned and I always will remember what happened.

Looking back, I can remember myself as arrogant, thinking I was invincible, due to the shelter my parents had once created for me. One thing I failed to do was to "smell the cheese often" in order to "know when it is getting old." What was happening was my surroundings gradually were being destroyed from the inside. After my parents divorced and my once mentoring and loving father, decided to pack up and leave for the other side of the country, I was left with absolute freedom. With this new freedom, I decided I should belong to a group of more popular kids who also had this kind of freedom; a group, I now realize, was the wrong crowd. This was very childish because while I thought I was having fun, I was also forgetting my childhood roots and my parents' careful upbringing of me. Life slowly became horrible and without notice, I became more alone than I had ever felt as an only child living with my parents. I dropped out of school my sophomore year in hopes of finding something better and new, but I did not. For some reason I grabbed on to life very tightly, probably because "the more important your cheese is to you the more you want to hold on to it," and my life was very important to me no matter how bad it was. Change was something I feared to do; and whether or not I believed it, it was inevitable.

One day life became so awful that I instinctively turned to my mother and grandmother, their solution was to change everything so change I did. "He had to admit that the biggest inhibitor to change lives within yourself, and that nothing gets better until you change." This is something that had to be realized, and luckily enough I realized it quickly and acted upon it. "Movement in a new direction helps you find new cheese." This I learned is very true, not only did my group of friends change, but I changed my ideas and morals as well. Turning my troublemaking comrades into a group of new faces and highly respected students. Anyone can say, "Woe is me," but only a select few can do something about their troubles; I fought and continue to fight valiantly in the battle against ignorance. Establishing personal goals and finding new meanings in life are what I use for motivation and personal will power. I became very enthusiastic, striving as hard as I could for perfection. In school, the only grades I told my self I would accept were A's, and I was more determined and enthusiastic about college as ever. I dug

(continued)

(continued)

up old sports and pushed my self as hard as I could, my Jr. Year I went to a wrestling tournament and climbed my way to third place in my weight class after not being on a team for two years. I fell in love with victory, and in hopes of embracing my feelings, I found faith and was confirmed as a catholic. Believing in my self, urged me to spread my wings, and finally take flight.

Finally, after years of fighting I was finally free from my own self-created mental prison. Achieving my goals was an extraordinary glory filled victory, which finally showed me my hard work had paid off; I finally found new cheese. The first marking period of my senior year, I was one of very few students in my class to have straight A's and receive the words "high honors" on their report card. In addition to that, I received an award for my efforts in English. Ever since, I have not been able to stride through the hallway of school without recognition from peers, teachers, faculty, and school administrators for either achievement. What I realize now is I saw what I was, I wanted to change, I worked hard, and I did it, I was successful. After achieving my goals, I did not allow myself to slip, for I made more goals to push my self even harder, because I cannot forget I still have a bright future in front of me.

Over the past few years, I have learned many lessons, but the most important one I learned from my faith, every one deserves a second chance because god is loving and <u>forgiving</u>. Right now I consider my self a changed man, a man of new cheese, a self-aware and active citizen who is capable and ready for college. The best advice ever given to me is, "you choose your own path." These words I live by.

—Brandon W., The College of Saint Rose

No Fear of Any Challenge

Nicholas's advice appears under the heading of his first essay in this chapter, "Why This School?"

Required personal essay.

Pectus excavatum, a condition that occurs in 1 out of every 1000 people, is cosmetically unappealing, restricts breathing, and reduces athletic performance; lucky me, I had it. In medical terms, it is the abnormal growth of the cartilage connecting the sternum to the ribs, so it grows inward instead of flat. In layman's terms, it looked like I was punched, so hard in the chest, it left a dent; a dent so deep that I could literally eat a bowl of cereal out of my thorax. Sounds attractive, huh?

© JIST Works

So, I had the option of getting my breastbone surgically "popped out" and reinforced with a steel bar; it was probably going to hurt, but I chose to do it anyway. At the hospital, I was led, scantily clad, into the operating room. The doctors, decked out in blue scrubs, told me to lie down on the black-cushioned operating table surrounded by large, expensive-looking machines and sharp pointy objects attached to wires; it was reminiscent of something found in an old Frankenstein movie. A thin layer of moisture began to gather on my forehead as I looked around. The doctors were taking their respective stations. A black mask was placed over my mouth and I began to feel as if someone was turning the dimmer switch on my brain.

"Okay, we have to do this while you're still mostly awake, give me your arm," said the anesthesiologist. I felt a slight poke, followed by the sliding of a wide needle under the skin of my right forearm. It slid back out. It figures they missed with the I.V. the first time, darn my narrow veins. Then, it was all black.

As I was resuming consciousness, the remaining anesthesia didn't allow me to open my eyes for more than ¼ of a second at a time; my speech would not return for another hour. I could perceive the distinct feeling that an overweight, stubborn grizzly bear had taken a seat on my body right below the neckline. The pressure was so great I emitted groans "resembling Chewbacca from Star Wars," according to my parents.

My chest now looked "normal." Dressing covered two small incisions beneath each breast where a custom-fitted metal bar ran under my sternum and was wired to my ribs on either side. Imagine your torso being squeezed by a vise and inflated like a balloon simultaneously; that's how I felt. I had oxygen and morphine at the press of a button (every 6 minutes). Thank the Lord for that button. Basic things such as swallowing, walking, lying down, and especially sitting up were now great chores. Thankfully, things got better with time, as my hospital stay was only four days. Four years later, and two years after removing the bar, my chest looks much better, and I am happy. I never once regret having surgery. Whenever something seems difficult, I can look back on this experience and say with confidence that I have been through worse pain and conquered it.

—Nicholas M., Tufts University

Be Inspired

This talented and interesting group of students has offered many creative and unique approaches to capturing the essence of who they are. You should feel empowered to meet this challenge head-on!

Good luck.

© JIST Works

Appendix

The Admission Professionals Who Contributed to This Book

These admission professionals generously provided their time and collective wisdom in thoroughly detailing the different admission practices used at these fine schools throughout the United States. In addition, the majority of these individuals spoke from a depth of admissions experience acquired over individual careers that approached 25 or more years in some instances—at other excellent universities and colleges around the country. For their able and ready assistance and enthusiasm for this project, I am most grateful.

Mr. Gil J. Villanueva
Dean of Admissions
Brandeis University
Office of Admissions, MS 003
415 South St.
Waltham, MA 02454
(781) 736-3501
gvillnva@brandeis.edu

Mr. Don Bishop
Associate Vice President for
Enrollment Management
Creighton University
2500 California Plaza
Omaha, NE 68178
(402) 280-2162
donbishop@creighton.edu

Ms. Jean Jordan
Interim Dean of Admission
Emory University
200 Bois Feuiellet Jones Center
Atlanta, GA 30322
(800) 727-6036
jean.jordan@emory.edu

Mr. Vince Cuseo
Dean of Admission
Occidental College
1600 Campus Rd.
Los Angeles, CA 90041
(323) 259-2700
vcuseo@oxy.edu

Mr. Paul Marthers
Dean of Admission
Reed College
Office of Admission
3203 SE Woodstock Blvd.
Portland, OR 97202
(503) 777-7510
marthers@reed.edu

Mrs. E. Jeanne Jenkins
Director, Strategic Initiatives
Rensselaer Admissions
Rensselaer Polytechnic Institute
110 8th St.
Troy, NY 12180
(518) 276-6216
jenkie@rpi.edu

Mr. Chris Muñoz
Vice President for Enrollment
Rice University
Admission Office-MS 17
P.O. Box 1892
Houston, TX 77251-1892
(713) 348-7423
chris.munoz@rice.edu

Mr. Richard Zeiser
Dean of Admission
University of Hartford
200 Bloomfield Ave.
West Hartford, CT 06117
(860) 768-4296
zeiser@hartford.edu

Mr. Eric Simonelli
Admission Advisor
University of Rhode Island
14 Upper College Rd.
Kingston, RI 02881
(401) 874-5351
esimonelli@mail.uri.edu

Douglas L. Christiansen, Ph.D.
Associate Provost for
Enrollment and Dean of
Admissions
Vanderbilt University
2201 West End Ave.
221 Kirkland Hall
Nashville, TN 37240
(615) 322-2111
douglas.christiansen@
vanderbilt.edu

© JIST Works

Index

© JIST Works

© JIST Works

© JIST Works

© JIST Works

© JIST Works